THIS BOOK BELONGS
TO Wizard

THE ART OF
MODERN
CONJURING

THE ART OF MODERN CONJURING

FOR WIZARDS OF ALL AGES

PROFESSOR HENRI GARENNE

GRAMERCY BOOKS
NEW YORK

This 2004 edition is published by Gramercy Books, an imprint of Random
House Value Publishing, a division of Random House, Inc., New York, by
arrangement with Crown Publishers, a division of Random House, Inc.

Gramercy is a registered trademark and the colophon is
a trademark of Random House, Inc.

Random House
New York • Toronto • London • Sydney • Auckland
www.randomhouse.com

Design by Maggie Hinders

Originally published in 1886 by Ward, Lock & Co.

Printed and bound in the United States

Library of Congress Cataloging-in-Publication Data

Garenne, Henri.
The art of modern conjuring : for wizards of all ages / Henri Garenne.
p. cm.
Originally published: London : Ward, Lock, and Co., 1886.
ISBN 0-517-22355-4
1. Magic tricks. I.Title.

GV1547.G29 2004
794.8—dc22
2003067634

ISBN 0-517-22355-4

10 9 8 7 6 5 4 3 2 1

CONTENTS

CHAPTER 3

Tricks with Cards

CHAPTER 4

Tricks with Coins

CHAPTER 5

Tricks with Rings

CHAPTER 6

Tricks with Handkerchiefs

CHAPTER 7

Tricks with Balls

CHAPTER 8

Tricks with Hats

CHAPTER 9

Miscellaneous Tricks

CHAPTER 10
Stage Tricks and Illusions

CHAPTER 11

Spiritualistic Illusions, Séances, and Manifestations

CHAPTER 12

Thought Reading

CHAPTER 13

Conclusion 202

THE ART OF
MODERN
CONJURING

CHAPTER 1

INTRODUCTION

The Author's Views and Intentions

Having devoted much time to the study and practice of the art of Conjuring and Illusions, I have determined to write this treatise upon the "dark" art. Conjuring is an art that has been known for many ages; and people were foolish enough to believe in those days, that the performer, or *magician*, had dealings with a certain dark gentleman whom we will not name. However, people of the present day are getting more enlightened; and although they see something done beyond their ken, yet they know it is only a piece of deception or sleight of hand on the part of the performers.

I have written this work not as an exposure of the art of Conjuring and Magic, but simply to act as a guide for amateurs and young beginners; therefore I shall enumerate many tricks and illusions that my young friends can perform at home amongst their numerous friends. In addition to this, I shall also enumerate those tricks and illusions which demand a larger amount of room, and also require specially constructed apparatus; such tricks the amateur would do well not to attempt, as they are only suitable for performance on a stage. I shall give a description of most of the numerous tricks and illusions as performed by most of the leading "wizards" of the past and present day. I shall also give a detailed account of many of the so-called spiritualistic illusions, manifestations, and séances, also a few hints and remarks upon the so-called latest novelty, thought-reading. My intention in these pages is to touch on sleight of hand generally, as well as other more particular and effective tricks and illusions. The reader, if he follows diligently the instructions that I will give him, will be able in a short time to astonish his numerous friends with his acquired knowledge. Of course, he cannot expect to be a Robert Houdin, a Professor Anderson, or a Robert Heller in a week, a month, or even a year, because a wizard is not to be made in a day. And the student will do well to commence the same as in learning the art of music or anything else, and begin at the beginning, with simple things first, and practice with diligence and perseverance until he attains the much coveted dexterity. Simple tricks, if performed neatly, have oftentimes a brilliant effect, and gain more applause from your audience than the performance of some more particular and costly trick.

Rules to Be Remembered

The first rule to be borne in mind is this: *Never tell your audience beforehand what you are going to do.* If you do so, the chances are that the spectators will then detect how you do such a trick, as their vigilance will be on the alert.

It next follows as a second rule: *Never perform the same trick twice before the same audience.* The best trick loses half its effect by repetition; besides which, the audience would know precisely what was coming, and would be on the alert to find out at what point you cheated their eyes on the first occasion.

If you get an encore, a little tact will always get you out of your difficulty; and when you have become thoroughly proficient in the art, you will then be able to find many ways of altering the working of a certain trick, in the variation and combination of ways and means of causing a given article to vanish and of reproducing a given article.

The student must cultivate the art of talking, from the first commencement, and to be able to use his eyes and hands independently, because in working or doing any trick, the performer must be talking to his audience, looking at them steadfastly, never once casting his eyes down toward his hands. I might say that the most effective way for the student to practice is to stand in front of a looking glass, where he can form a better idea if a looker-on can detect what he is doing.

This he will find most particularly useful in practicing card tricks.

Before proceeding to the practice of the art of Magic, a short description is necessary of a few of the appliances which are in constant use and requisition by every one who practices the art of Conjuring.

Of these, first in order comes—

The Magician's Wand

This is a light rod, about fifteen inches long and three-quarters of an inch in diameter. It may be of any material, but is generally made of ebony. It is decorated in any manner the owner may fancy. To the uninitiated, it may appear a mere piece of affectation on the part of the performer; but such is not the case. Without his wand, a magician would be at a loss on many occasions what to do, because the wand affords a plausible pretext for many necessary movements, which would, without its use, appear very awkward, and thereby sharpen the vigilance of the audience at, perhaps, the most critical portion of the trick. If the performer wishes to hold anything concealed in his hand, by holding the wand in the same hand, he can keep it closed without the slightest suspicion. If it is necessary, as frequently happens, to walk to the table to get rid of, or to pick up, any desired article, the mere taking up or putting down of the wand affords the required opportunity.

I should always advise the student to cultivate the habitual use of the wand. With its use the performer can, according to his professed character, cause a magical transformation, by using it, and touching daintily the articles he is supposed to be operating on, thus leading his audience to believe that such a change did actually take place at that particular moment, instead of having been secretly effected at an earlier period.

The Magician's Tables

It is generally the practice to have three tables when performing, one center table and two smaller or side tables. Of course it is not necessary to use the three, as in many instances the performer can do all he requires with the one center table.

There are many kinds of conjuring tables in use, being specially made, and fitted with various concealed traps, pistons, etc. This kind of table is, however, chiefly used for stage performances. For the student, however, who intends starting only with simple and minor tricks, an ordinary table will do, but with this difference, that the legs should be six or eight inches longer than the legs of an ordinary table. The required height could be obtained by putting firm blocks of the necessary height, with a depression made in the top of each of them in which to put the bottom of the table legs, thus making it firm and preventing it from slipping off the blocks.

At the back of the table, it is necessary to have a shelf or ledge fixed, this shelf to be six or eight inches in width, extending nearly from end to end.

Such a shelf could be made portable, to enable the performer to fix it on any table, by means of short thumbscrews.

This shelf is technically known as the *servante*, and should be covered with a thick woolen cloth or green baize, to deaden the sound of anything falling upon it. When it is not possible to fix a *servante*, a table having a drawer in one side can be used, the side with the drawer in to be away from the audience, this upon occasion will make a tolerably fair *servante*.

Over this table should be thrown a small cover, fastened at the back edge with a couple of drawing pins, to prevent its slipping. This cloth should hang down a few inches from the top of the table, enabling the audience to look right under the table. This class of table will do very well for amateurs to use, until they get more initiated into the art of Stage Conjuring, in which case they would require to use proper conjuring tables or tables fitted with a combination of traps, pistons, etc., and such can be had either with ornamental fronts or plain. As regards the two small side tables, or *guéridons*, or stands for candles, lamps, etc., they are made either with plain tops, or can be made fitted with traps, similar to the center table; if the latter, they are very useful for getting rid of any article or articles in the course of working a trick. Many performers use only plain tables, and they are either brought forward or put back, to assist in the period of working some tricks, as they are much more convenient to use than the larger table. The height of the center table, to an extent, depends upon the height of the performer; the shelf or *servante* at the back of the center table should be just high enough from the flooring to be on a level with the hands of the performer when his arms hang by his side; and the top of the table should be about six inches higher than this. The performer will find that this will enable him to pick up or put down any article without stooping or altering the position of his body in the least.

One of the first tasks of the novice should be to acquire the power of quickly picking up or laying down any article on the *servante* without any corresponding motion of the body, and especially to abstain from looking down at his hands, because if the audience once suspects that he has a secret receptacle behind his table, half the novelty of his tricks is thenceforth destroyed.

A small oblong box, well padded with wadding, or half filled with bran, should be placed on the *servante:* it will be found useful in getting rid of small articles, such as eggs, oranges, coins, rings, etc.; and they can be dropped into the box without causing the slightest sound, or attracting attention. Be particular, in setting the table ready before commencing a performance, not to have a lot of unnecessary articles on the table, as it looks unsightly; and the performer must place the various articles he will require on the *servante* in such position that he can walk up to the table and pick such articles up without once looking down. With a little practice, the performer will be able to do this easily and without attracting the slightest attention.

The next most important thing is—

The Magician's Dress

It was formerly the custom of conjurers to wear a long flowing robe, embroidered with strange figures. This style of dress allowed the performer to conceal a quantity of large-sized articles. However, that style of dress has now been long discarded, and the costume of a magician of the present day is an ordinary evening dress suit. Of course the effect is materially heightened, on account of the comparative scantiness of such a costume, which appears to allow of no space for concealing various articles. In reality, this dress is specially provided with large and deep pockets, called *profondes*, for the reception of concealed articles. In the tails of the coat are placed two large pockets, from six to eight inches in depth and about eight inches across, with the opening slanting slightly downwards from the center to the side. The performer can thus, by merely dropping his hand to his side, let fall any article into the *profonde* on that side, or take anything from thence in a like manner; the action is so natural that the audience never observe it, more especially if the performer slightly turns that side of his body away from the audience. In addition to this, some performers have a deep pocket made on the inside of the breast of the coat on either side, being made according to the fancy of the wearer; such pockets are especially useful in producing globes of goldfish.

In the trousers a couple of small pockets (styled *pochettes*) are made, one behind each thigh. These are more generally used for production only. Other pockets can also be added, according to the fancy of the wearer, but the above generally suffice.

As regards the waistcoat, it will be found a very great convenience to have an elastic band stitched around the lower edge of the waistcoast; this makes it press tightly round the waist, and such articles as cards or a handkerchief may be slipped under, without the least fear of their falling.

If the performer has his dress made and fitted as above, he will be able to produce and get rid of, instantaneously, many articles which are too large to be palmed; and with a slight turn of his body he can get rid of an article with one hand, and produce the substitute with the other.

Talking to the Audience

Before concluding these introductory remarks, I may add that it is most desirable for the performer to be able to use his tongue fluently and talk glibly at all times, because it takes off the attention of the audience from his movements. Thus the performer is enabled, while he is talking, to effect the various changes he requires. It is not well to represent that you intend doing such-and-such great tricks, but to tell your audience that you will amuse them with a few *simple* tricks; and you will invariably find that the audience are more astonished, because, expecting to see something simple, it strikes them all with wonder and amazement when a more elaborate trick is performed. With this advice, I shall draw my introductory remarks to a close, and get on to the more serious matter of Tricks and Illusions.

CHAPTER 2

HINTS ON PALMING

Preliminary Remarks

The first faculty which the novice should seek to acquire is that of "palming," or holding an object in the open hand by the mere contraction of the palm, without the audience being able to observe it. In practicing the art of palming, the novice will do well, as I stated before, to stand in front of a looking glass, in which position he must practice diligently to palm such articles as a pack of cards, oranges, eggs, watches, rings, coins, and even a pocket handkerchief.

In palming a pocket handkerchief, you must take it in your left hand, and commence rolling it into a small ball with the right, and then quietly make a pass, and apparently take the folded handkerchief into your right hand, which should be immediately closed, to cause the audience to believe that the handkerchief is really held in that hand, and at the same time drop the left hand carelessly to the side, and the handkerchief, which is in reality in that hand, can then be easily gotten rid of by dropping it into the *profonde* on that side; or it can be produced from any particular place or object that the performer chooses.

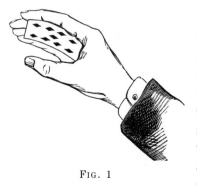

Fig. 1

In respect to cards, they cannot be palmed quite so easily, but should be held by the contraction of thumb at the bottom, and the slight contraction of the top joints of the fingers at the top of the cards, as shown in fig. 1.

It frequently happens, in the course of card tricks, that several cards will have to be palmed in that way, and in some cases half the deck; but of that I shall treat further on, when describing card tricks.

The novice will find that an egg can be very easily palmed without much practice; but he must be careful never to relax the grip or contraction of the palm when holding it, because the egg would invariably fall to the ground, thus opening the eyes of the audience as to where the egg has been concealed, thereby causing them to exert their utmost vigilance to endeavour to detect his modus operandi in his other tricks.

In commencing to palm coins, I should strongly recommend the novice to begin with a quarter, as that is more easily held than other coins; and when he has got thoroughly proficient in palming and making the various passes with that coin, he can proceed to practice with other coins, and if he is expert, he will soon be enabled to palm not only one, but many coins, and after a little practice he would be able to walk amongst his audience, and with dexterity to take coins from ladies' bonnets and hats, and from gentlemen's beards, hair, and coat sleeves, causing thereby a great deal of merriment amongst the spectators.

Modes and Methods of Palming: Palming Coins

I shall now proceed to explain the various ways and methods of palming. In the first place, take a quarter and lay it on the palm of your left hand, as in fig. 2. Now close the hand very slightly, and if you have the coin placed right, the contraction of the palm around its edges will hold it securely, as in fig. 3, and you can then move the hand and arm in

Fig. 2

any direction, without the slightest fear of its dropping; and you should next practice to move the fingers and use the hand easily and naturally, while the coin is still held as above; bear also in mind always to keep the inside of the palm either down or towards the body, because, if you failed to do so, you would expose the coin.

Fig. 3

Passes with Coins

I shall proceed with the various "passes," which all have the object of apparently transferring an article from one hand to the other, although the article is still retained in the hand it apparently just quitted.

First Pass. Take the coin in the right hand, between the second and third fingers and the thumb, as in fig. 4, sup-

FIG. 4

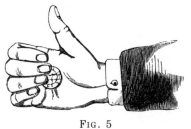

FIG. 5

ported by the fingers and steadied by the thumb. Now move the thumb and close the second and third fingers, with the coin on them, into the palm, as in fig. 5. If the coin was placed correctly, you will find that this motion puts it in exactly the same position as shown in fig. 3, when the fingers are again extended.

The novice should practice this with both the right and the left hand, until he can perform easily with either hand. When he has mastered the above, he should practice doing the same thing, in motion only, toward the left hand, which should meet it open, but which should close the moment the fingers of the right hand touch its palm, as though closing up upon the coin, and the left hand should thenceforth remain closed, as if retaining the coin, and the right hand should hang loosely open, as if empty, although in reality it is the hand which holds the coin. A judicious use of the wand will materially help in concealing the fact that the object is held in the right hand. For this purpose the performer should, before commencing the pass, place his wand carelessly under either right or left arm, as though to leave the free use of his hands. After the pass is made, the performer can then with an easy motion grasp the wand and draw it from under his arm, and retain it until he disposes of the coin, as may be necessary.

Second Pass. The pass about to be described is slightly easier than the first that I have mentioned, and can be sometimes substituted for it. Take the coin edgewise between the first and third fingers of the right hand, pressing the sides of those fingers against the edge of the coin, steadying it from behind with the middle finger, as in fig. 4. Carry the right toward the left, moving the thumb quickly over the face of the coin until the top joint passes its outer edge (see fig. 6); bend the thumb, and the coin will be securely nipped between the joint and the junction of the thumb with the hand (see fig. 7). As in the last pass, you must

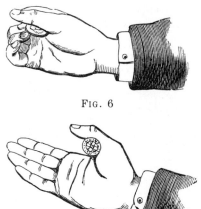

FIG. 6

FIG. 7

F<small>IG</small>. 8

close the left hand the moment the right hand touches it; and the right hand must then be held with the thumb bent slightly in towards the palm, to shield the coin from the view of the audience. This is a very rapid mode of palming, and if cleanly executed, the illusion is perfect.

Third Pass: "Le Tourniquet." This is an easy pass. Hold the left hand palm upward with the coin as in fig. 8. Next move the right hand toward the left hand, passing the thumb of the right hand under and the fingers over the coin, closing them just as they pass it. To the audience it appears as if you seized the coin with the thumb and fingers, but in reality, the moment the coin is covered by the fingers of

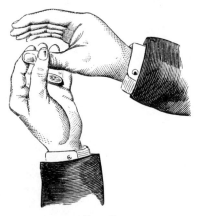

F<small>IG</small>. 9

right hand, you let it drop into the palm of the left (see fig. 9). You should then carry the right hand upward, after it leaves the left, following it with your eyes, leading the audience to believe that the coin is in that hand, thereby drawing away their attention from your left hand (see fig. 10). Let your left hand fall gently to your side, with the palm toward you, the fingers being slightly bent. The hollow thus made is sufficient to hold the coin.

This pass is especially available for small coins which cannot readily be palmed by ordinary means.

Fourth Pass: "La Pincette." This pass is very similar to the last. The coin is held (see fig. 11) between the thumb and the first and second fingers of the left hand. Then make the movement of taking it with the same fingers of the right hand, the back of the hand being kept toward the audience. The moment the coin is covered by the right hand, allow it to slip

FIG. 10

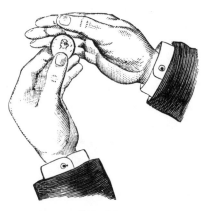

FIG. 11

gently down into the left palm, and immediately close the right hand and elevate it, as if containing the coin, letting the left hand drop gently to the side as described before.

There are many other kinds of passes, but those I have described the novice will find the most useful.

Cautions Respecting Passing

Bear in mind that these passes are not to be regarded as tricks, but only as certain processes to be used in the performance of certain tricks. The student should accustom himself *always to follow with his eyes the hand in which the object is supposed to be held;* by so doing he will naturally lead the eyes and minds of his audience in the same direction. When the student has thoroughly mastered these passes neatly with a single quarter, he should then practice with other coins of smaller size, and then with two, and afterwards increasing with a greater number, until he is thoroughly master of palming a large number of coins, which is necessary in the execution of certain tricks.

Utility of Passes

The passes described above can be employed not only to cause the disappearance of an article, but to secretly exchange it for a substitute of similar appearance. Such exchanges are in continual use in conjuring, and most of its marvels depend upon them, especially when executed neatly. When the performer has made such an exchange, the substitute should be left in the full sight of the audience, while the performer, having thus secretly gained possession of the original, disposes of it as may be necessary for the purpose of the trick he has in hand, and reproduces in many various ways, which I shall explain in describing different tricks.

Ringing

In concluding my remarks upon palming and passing—in conjurer's parlance, called "ringing"—if the student wishes to make a clever conjurer, he must practice these passes well, and if he can execute them neatly and with rapidity and dexterity, he will then find the remainder easily accomplished.

CHAPTER 3

TRICKS WITH CARDS

Cards and Cardplaying

Cards were invented in Spain, during the fourteenth century; but so great was the base practice of cardplaying in that generation, that in the year 1738, John I, King of Castile, commanded that cardplaying should be abolished in his kingdom. At the present day, many bad characters go in for swindling the unwary with cardplaying, such base, unprincipled fellows having, no doubt, learned how to pass and change various cards, and the poor innocent victim not knowing how easy it is for such characters to cheat them out of their hard-earned money. Cardplaying for money is a bad practice at any time, and my young readers will do well to keep away from it. My hints upon card tricks are not meant to teach the reader to cheat, but to amuse; and what is more amusing, on a long winter's evening, than to sit and watch an endless number of tricks in sleight of hand with cards? Amongst the conjurer's art, none will better repay the labor of the student than the magic of cards. It has the special advantage of being, in a very great measure, independent of time and place, the materials usually being procurable in every home. The majority of card tricks depend principally upon the personal address and dexterity of the performer, and such will be always highly esteemed by any audience.

Suitable Cards for Card Tricks

The performer in sleight of hand should accustom himself to the use of every kind of cards, as frequently only ordinary, full-sized playing cards are procurable. When, however, the performer can have his choice, he should select cards of a smaller and thinner make.

To Make the Pass

The effect of this piece of sleight of hand is to reverse the positions of the top and bottom halves of the pack, and to make those cards which formed the lower half of the pack come uppermost, which will of course bring the upper half to the bottom. This is a trick very often used by cardsharpers immediately after the cards have been cut, to replace them in the same position as they were before. There are various methods of producing this effect, some requiring one hand, and some both hands. These I will endeavor to describe in their due order.

1. First Method, with Both Hands. Hold the pack in the left hand lengthwise, with the face downward. In this position the thumb will be on the left side of the pack, and the four fingers on the other side. Insert the top joint of the little finger above those cards which are to be brought to the top of the pack (and which forms the lower half), and let the remaining three fingers close on the remaining cards, which are now uppermost (see fig. 12). Now advance the right hand and cover the pack. Grasp the lower portion of the pack lengthwise, between the second finger at the upper and the thumb at the lower end, the left thumb lying

FIG. 12

across the pack. Press the inner edge of the lower packet into the fork of the left thumb, so that they will be as in fig. 13. Next draw away the upper packet, by extending the fingers of the left hand, at the same time lifting up the outer edge of the lower packet till the edges of the packets just clear each other (as in fig. 14), when the act of merely closing the left hand will bring the two packets together as at first, except that they will have changed places. The student must do this very slowly at first. At the outset this task will no doubt be rather difficult, but after a little practice the student will find that he can execute this sleight with almost lightninglike rapidity. The student, when performing, must be particular *never to look toward his hands.*

2. Second Method, with Both Hands. Hold the pack in the left hand as directed before, and grasp the lower por-

FIG. 13

tion lengthwise as before, between the second finger at the upper, and the thumb at the lower end; move the left thumb a little below the pack, to be out of the way. Now slide the lower half of the pack slightly to the left, and the upper half to the right, till they just clear each other (see fig. 15), which

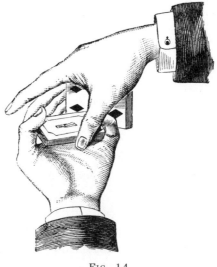

Fig. 14

will enable you to place what was the upper half undermost, or vice-versa. You must study to do this with the slightest

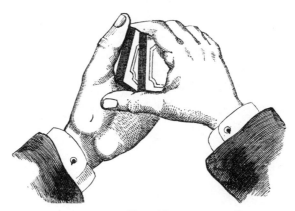

Fig. 15

possible movement, and to keep the hands together as much as possible.

3. Third Method, with Left Hand Only. Hold the cards in the left hand, and insert the third finger just above the cards that are to be brought to the top, and which form the lower half of the pack; close the remaining three fingers on the top of the pack as in fig. 12; but with the third finger inserted instead of the fourth. Extend the fingers, which will make the upper half of the pack describe a semicircle, as in fig. 16; at the same moment press the left top corner of the lower half downward with the thumb. This will cause the opposite end to tilt up, giving room, as you again close the fingers, for the upper half to fall into the lower place as shown in fig. 17. This method has a peculiarity which renders it useful in certain cases, because when the upper half describes a semicircle, as mentioned above, the bottom card of that half is brought to the view of the performer,

Fig. 16

although the audience only sees the backs. Such knowledge is at times very useful to the performer. A quick sweep of the arm from left to right, as the pass is being made, will materially assist in covering the transposition of the cards, and confuses the eyes of the spectator.

4. Fourth Method, with Either Hand. Take the pack in either hand, the backs of the cards against the palm;

FIG. 17

insert the third finger between the two halves of the pack, then draw the second and fourth fingers behind the pack. In

this position the upper half is held between the third, second, and fourth fingers. Clip the lower or front half at its two corners, between the thumb and first finger, as in fig. 18. Extend the second, third, and fourth fingers, which by so doing will carry with them the upper half of the pack. As soon as it clears the lower half, again close the fingers, which will bring the upper half to the bottom,

FIG. 18

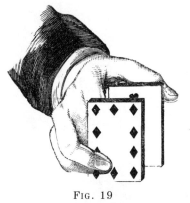

FIG. 19

as in fig. 19. This pass can be executed when the performer advances to place the pack of cards on his table.

5. *Fifth Method, with Right Hand.* This pass is usually performed in picking up the cards from the table, after they have been cut, and, as is usual, left in two heaps. The performer picks up the bottom half of the pack, but instead of picking them up in the ordinary way, he picks them up with the second, third, and fourth fingers underneath, and the first finger on the top of the cards. In placing them apparently upon the upper heap, he tilts up the right-hand edge of that heap with the tip of his first finger, and with the remaining fingers slides the heap he already holds underneath it, as in fig. 19, so that the cards are precisely the same as they were before the pack was cut. This sham mode of making a pass is very rarely used by conjurers, but is constantly done by cardsharpers.

To "Force" a Card

By this phrase is meant compelling a person to draw such a card as you desire, although he apparently has his own freedom of choice. Many performers use what are usually called a "forcing-pack," i.e., a pack in which all the cards are alike. Others use a pack of two or three different cards; for instance, for the well-known trick of the rising cards, the pack may consist of jack of hearts, queen of diamonds, and ace of clubs, one-third of each kind being put in to make up the pack.

Again, other performers use an ordinary pack of cards, but have the first four cards selected and placed on the top of the pack. The performer, stepping forward, requests one of the audience to shuffle the pack, holding the cards in his left hand and apparently toying with them with his right hand. As he is about to hand the cards to the person to shuffle them, he adroitly palms with his right hand the cards he has placed in position, handing the remainder of the pack to the person to shuffle, explaining to the audience that he uses no prepared cards, and calling attention to the fact that every card in the pack is different.

When the cards are well shuffled, the performer receives them in his left hand, bringing it upward; at the same time he covers the top of the pack with his right hand, thereby enabling him to return the prepared cards to the top of the pack.

Now, holding the pack opened slightly fan-shape and nipping the cards tightly at the bottom corners, he presents the pack to some person in the audience to select one, purposely having the cards he wishes to be drawn nearest to the person who is selecting. This card will of course come forth easily; but if the person should attempt to pick a different card he will find that he cannot draw it easily, and will pick upon another which he can draw easily. The performer, directly that he notices the person intends to select the wrong card, tightens his grasp upon the corners of the cards, thereby preventing the possibility of its being drawn.

This is by far the best method of "forcing a card," as the pack can always be handed for examination, to show that the cards are not all alike.

A moderate degree of practice will make the student quite proficient in being able to force the desired card.

To Make "False Shuffles"

False shuffles have generally some object in view, or reason for so doing, the first being designed to keep in view a particular card, or cards; and the second to keep the pack in prearranged order. These are merely shuffles in appearance, all the cards being brought back into the very same position that they occupied previous to being shuffled.

First Method of Making a False Shuffle. There are several methods, the first being to keep a particular card in view. Take the pack into the left hand. If the card you wish to keep in view is not already on the top, then insert the little finger of the left hand just above that card, and make the pass to enable you to bring it to the top; then transfer this card to the right hand, and slide the remaining cards onto it by successive parcels of six or eight cards, one above the other. The known card will now be at the bottom of the pack. Take the pack again in the left hand, slide off three or four of the top cards into your right hand, and place the remainder of cards in parcels of six or eight as before, alternately above and below these top cards, till you come to the last card, which is the selected one, and which you can place above or below as occasion may require. If you wish to keep three or four cards in view, the mode of operation is exactly the same, except that you must treat those cards throughout as a single card, and accordingly keep them together.

Second Method of Making a False Shuffle. The second method to retain the whole pack in a prearranged order is as follows: Take the pack into the left hand, slide off with the thumb of that hand five or six of the top cards into the right hand, and place the remainder of the cards by parcels of five or six at a time (apparently) alternately above and below these first cards, as in the usual mode of shuffling. I said *apparently*, but in reality, although you make the motion of placing every alternate packet above the cards in your right hand, you do not leave it there, but draw it back with your thumb onto the top of the cards in your left hand, and then place it by your next movement *under* the cards in your right hand, thus making the pack as it was at first, as the cards in the left hand, instead of being placed alternately above and below those in the right hand, are all really placed below.

To "Palm" a Card

Hold the pack in your left hand, and bring the card you desire to palm (either by the pass or otherwise) to the top of the pack. With the thumb, push the top card until it projects slightly beyond the edge of the pack. With the third finger of the left hand, press the card upward into your right hand, which should slightly close over it, held as shown in fig. 1 in my remarks on palming. You may let your hand fall easily to your side, and can then offer the pack to be shuffled.

To return the card to the pack is a very easy matter, as the mere action of taking the cards from the left into the right hand returns the card to the top. If the card should retain its bent form from being held in that position in your hand, it may readily be straightened by ruffling the cards slightly with the left hand. If the performer has a large hand, he will find no difficulty in being able to "palm" a complete deck of cards.

To "Change" a Card

Some of the most brilliant tricks in card conjuring are done by the aid of this sleight, by which a card exhibited is apparently transformed to another one. There are several modes of doing this, but I shall describe only two. Hold the pack in the left hand as though you intended to deal out the cards. In your right hand hold the card to be changed between the first and second fingers. The card into which it is intended to be changed should previously be placed (secretly) on the top of the pack. With your left thumb, push this card slightly beyond the remaining cards, then bring your hands together for an instant, and immediately place the card in the right hand *under* the pack (the second, third, and fourth fingers opening to receive it, and the remaining finger making way for it as soon as it reaches the pack). Simultaneously with this movement, close the thumb and first finger of the right hand upon the card projecting from the top of the pack, and as you separate your hands, carry with them the card in place of the one which was held originally in the right hand.

A slight turn of the body, or a rapid movement or sweep of the right hand, will assist in covering the momentary bringing together of the hands.

Another method, with One Hand Only. Take the pack in

the left hand, face downward, as if about to deal them out. Have the card to be changed on the top, and the card for which it is to be changed next below it. With your thumb, push forward the top card to about the extent of half its width, letting it rest on the tips of the fingers, thus leaving one-half of the second card exposed. By a reverse movement of the thumb, draw back the second card until its outer edge is clear of the inner edge of the topmost card. With the thumb, press the second card slightly downward, so as to bring its opposite edge just above the level of the top card; then, with a sharp movement, push it back into its place, but this time above instead of below the top card, by this means quickly changing the relative positions of the two cards.

To Get Sight of a Drawn Card

The most expert operator cannot always force a required card; therefore it is necessary to be provided with a remedy in case of such a contretemps. Get some person in the audience to draw a card, and when he has done so, ask him to return it to the pack, which you offer to him for that purpose, in your left hand, spreading the pack out in the shape of a fan, in order that he can place it where he pleases. When he has done so, slip the little finger of the left hand *below* it, and then close the fan together; you now hold the pack in the left hand, with the little finger inserted below the chosen card, the remaining three fingers being on the top of the pack. Offer someone the cards to shuffle, at the same moment slightly straightening the fingers. The effect of this movement will be to lift up the top packet of cards, thus opening the pack bookwise, toward yourself, thereby exposing the lowest card of the top packet, which is the one you desired to see, to ascertain what card it really was. After so doing, close the hand quickly, and get some person to shuffle the pack, which, when returned to you, you open fanwise, but this time, with the faces of the cards toward you, and pretending to scan them over, pick out the chosen card and hand it to the person who drew it, asking him if it is the right card. A variety of other tricks can be executed in connection with the above, as the performer knows the selected card.

To Draw Back a Card

Between the first finger and thumb of the left hand, hold the pack upright, with the backs towards the palm, the thumb and finger being at about the middle of each side of the pack. Moisten the third finger, and let it rest on the face of the cards. In this position, by moving the third finger, you can draw the bottom card back about an inch below the other cards, thereby leaving exposed a corresponding portion of the next card. This card, of course, when drawn, appears to the audience to be the bottom card of the pack, when in reality it is not.

To Make Four Cards Change from Eights to Twos, and from Black to Red

For this trick you want specially prepared cards, the backs the same as those you have in ordinary use, but the faces to be as in fig. 20. Place these three cards privately at the bottom of pack, and begin by remarking that you will show the company a good trick with four eights and the two of diamonds.

FIG. 20

Take the pack in your hand and pick out the four genuine eights, and hand them to be examined. While this is being done, insert the little finger of your left hand between the three bottom cards (which are the prepared ones) and the rest of the pack. When the eights are returned, place them carelessly on the top of the pack (having, however, the eight of clubs uppermost), and then hand the two of diamonds to be examined. While this is being done, make the pass, and bring the three bottom cards to the top. The two of diamonds being handed back, lay it on the table, and then take off the four top cards from the pack and spread them fanwise on the table, and they will appear to be four eights, as shown in fig. 21. The top card (eight of clubs) is alone completely visible, one half of each the other cards being covered. Insert now the two of diamonds behind the eight of clubs, and then put that card upon the table. Close the cards again together, and spread them out again fanwise, but this time with the opposite ends outward, when they will appear to be the four twos, as in fig. 22. You can make other

FIG. 21

FIG. 22

changes with these cards by moving the positions of two of the cards, that is, by turning the opposite ends around. They can be made to appear all black one moment, and the next to be all red, by simply changing the position of the cards; of course, if they are to be all black, the eight of clubs must be uppermost, or if they are to be red, then the clubs must be removed, and the two of diamonds substituted.

These cards are to be procured at any conjuring emporium.

To Nail a Chosen Card to the Wall

Get a sharp pin, and place it anywhere where it will not attract attention, and yet be ready to your hand when required. Get some person to draw a card, and ask him to return it to the pack, make the pass, and bring it to the top, palm it, and offer the pack to be shuffled. While this is done, place your hand containing the card carelessly over the pin, so as to bring the center of the card over the pin, gently press the card, so as to make the point of the pin just penetrate it. When the pack is returned, place the palmed card upon the top, thus pressing home the pin, which will now project through the back of the card. Get some person to say in what part of the room they would like the chosen card to appear when selected, stand two or three feet off, and throw the cards sharply, backs foremost, against it, doing the best to make them strike as flat as possible. The selected card will appear pinned to the woodwork, and the remaining cards will fall to the floor. A little practice is necessary before the student can do this with dexterity.

To Change the Ace of Clubs to the Ace of Diamonds

For this illusion you must procure two cards alike, such as the ace of clubs. Cut the ace of clubs very carefully from one of these cards and rub a little soap upon the back of it, and carefully place it over the ace of diamonds, which it will cover entirely. Have the card placed on your *servante* so as to be readily picked up. Commence by bringing forward a pack of cards, and get some person to draw a card, which should be forced, and necessarily the ace of clubs. Request the person to notice the card and to replace it in the pack, then make the pass and bring it to the top, palming it. Hand the cards to be shuffled, and while this is being done, walk toward your table, apparently to pick up your wand, but at the same time quickly dropping the real ace of clubs onto the *servante*, and pick up the prepared card, which you palm as before. Now step forward to take with your left hand the pack from the person who shuffled them, quickly covering them with your right, thereby bringing the prepared card to the top of the pack. Apparently cut them and, picking out the prepared card, show it to your audience, and ask if that was the card selected. Place the pack upon the table, still retaining the prepared card in your hand, holding it face downward, and inform your audience that you intend to change the card you hold, at the same time showing it, into the ace of diamonds, by merely touching it with your wand; at the same moment draw your right hand under the card, scratching off with the tips of the fingers the false ace of clubs. With your right take your wand, and slightly touching it, command it to change, and upon exhibiting the card, it will, to the astonishment of your audience, appear to have been really changed into the ace of diamonds. This illusion requires a little practice before the student can do it neatly.

The Rising Card Trick

This is one of the best card tricks, and its origin may be traced to the famous Robert Houdin. There are many modes of working this trick, with various kinds of apparatus, some, indeed, very expensive; but, notwithstanding, this clever illusion can be prepared at a very small cost and outlay, and is every bit as effective and startling to the audience. In fact, many performers of the present day prefer to use the more simple apparatus, as hereinafter described, to the expensive and elaborate pieces of mechanism purchased at conjuring shops.

Get a small box, made either of thin wood or stout cardboard, large enough to hold a pack of cards, but only about three-quarters the length of a card in depth. Paint or paper this case black, and to the bottom glue or nail a long round piece of wood, about six inches long. Next obtain an ordinary black wine bottle, and half fill it with sand or water to enable it to stand steady. Insert into the neck of the bottle the piece of wood fixed to the bottom of the small box for holding the pack of cards. Now have a wood box made about eight inches square, open at the bottom, and on the top fix four small pieces of wood to keep the bottle in position when placed on the top. Paper or paint the box according to your fancy; bore a small hole in the top of the box toward the back, and another hole, close to the bottom, in the back of the box, or that part of the box away from the audience, as shown in fig. 23. Now get two packs of cards, and draw from each pack the king of clubs, jack of hearts, eight of spades, six of diamonds, and six of clubs. Next get about five yards of black silk. Place the pack of cards in the box, putting one end of the silk between two of the cards, the remainder of the silk lying across the top of the other cards, and hanging over the back. Now take the jack of hearts and push it gently down into the pack, of course taking the silk thread down with it; next place the king of clubs, taking care, however, not to place it exactly next to the jack, but to have one or two cards between; press the king gently down, taking the black silk thread as before, and repeat this until you have placed all the cards in position required; now draw the silk thread over the back of the case, and pass the end of the thread through the hole in the top of the box, and out again at the bottom hole of box at back, giving this end to your assistant behind your curtain. When the bottle is fixed on the box, as in fig. 23, the illusion will be perfect and ready for use, being placed on the center of your table, and your assistant being in readiness behind the curtain, thread in hand. Now take a pack of cards and, placing the other set of cards selected, and similar to those placed in position in the case on your table, put them in the center, and request some person to draw a card, taking

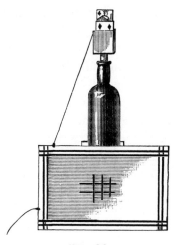

FIG. 23

care to force those you wish drawn, and so on until you have the required cards drawn. Having forced the five cards, request the persons who drew them not to forget their names, and, walking to your table, place the drawn cards in the case, taking care, however, to put them behind the front card in the case, which card the audience can see, thus apparently to your audience placing them in the center of the pack. Now tell your audience that you command the cards selected to rise out of the pack; and, turning to the pianist, if there is one, ask for a little music, and at the same moment your assistant will gently pull the thread, causing the last card placed in position to rise slowly out of the pack. When the card has nearly come to the top, say "Stop." This will be the signal for your assistant to cease pulling. Walk to the case, take out the card, and place it on a small tray; then repeat the same to each of the other cards, calling upon each of them by name to appear, until you come to the last card placed in position for rising, which will be the jack of hearts. When you command the jack to rise, be sure your assistant does not pull the thread. As the jack does not appear, turn to your audience and say, "I have forgotten, this gentleman is rather particular; I should have said, 'Please, John, will you jump up.'" Turn again toward the case, and repeat that sentence, and when you come to the word "jump," your assistant must pull the thread very sharply, and by so doing it will cause the card to spring quickly out of the pack and to fall on the table. This last pull on the part of your assistant will also pull the thread clear of the case, in fact, drawing it completely away. Take all the cards that have risen from the case, one by one, and show them to your audience, asking them if they are not the same cards that were selected. You can then lift the small case from the bottle, and, taking out the cards, hand it for examination, the audience, of course, failing to discover the trick. This a very grand and effective trick, and cannot fail to mystify any audience if correctly performed, and a little practice will soon make the student expert.

As regards the cards, many performers use a forcing pack for this experiment (see my earlier remarks on forcing a card), but it looks much better, and makes the illusion more perfect, if the audience sees you are using a genuine pack, which you can show them, holding the cards up fanwise.

Catching a Card on the Point of a Sword

For this trick you require a specially constructed sword. It is similar in appearance to an ordinary small sword, with a three-sided rapier blade as shown in fig. 24, but altered to suit this trick, the tip or end of the blade being cut off about half an inch from the extreme point, as in fig. 25. This end is fastened by a piece of thin black elastic, passed through a small hole made for that purpose, and through a corresponding hole in the top of the other part of blade, and running down the inside or hollow part of the blade to the hilt or handle. The tension of the elastic keeps the tip in its position, but it can, however, be drawn away as far as the elastic will permit, and when released it flies back to its proper position. On the same side of the hilt or handle is fixed a flat oblong piece of tin, with its side edges folded over about half an inch on each side, in such a manner as to form a receptacle for the card, as shown in fig. 26.

You now select a certain card, for instance the four of dia-

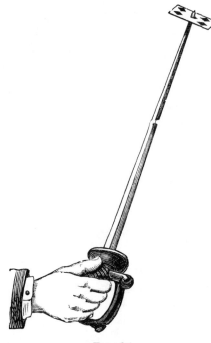

FIG. 24

monds, and with a penknife make a small slit in the center of the card, and put the tip of the sword completely through the hole thus made, and, drawing it well down, place it with the card in the case in the hilt of the sword. This is now ready, so place it on your table in such a manner that the audience cannot see its mechanism.

Now take a pack of cards in your hands and request some person to select a card, taking care, however, to force a similar card to that fixed in the sword hilt. Request the person to replace the card in the pack, and as he does so, make the pass and bring it to the top, palming it. Hand the pack to this person to shuffle, and while he is doing so, secretly drop the palmed card into your *profonde*.

Next, request this person to step forward with the cards, and to throw them into the air at your command. Step to your table and grasp your sword firmly, taking care, however, not to release

FIG. 25

the card until you are ready, and be sure to keep the back of your hand toward the audience.

Now tell the person who holds the cards to throw them into the air when you count three. At that word he throws them upward, and at the same moment you thrust the sword quickly among the cards as they are falling, at the same time releasing the movable tip, which, as it flies instantly to its proper position, carries the card that was concealed in the hilt with it, by which means it appears as if it was transfixed, as in fig. 24. The sudden movement in making the lunge with

Fig. 26

the sword, coupled with the falling cards, completely covers the rapid flight of the card from the hilt to the point. Tear the card from off the point of the sword and hand it to the person who drew it, at the same moment placing your sword on the table.

The person can then gather up the cards, and examine them, when he will naturally find that the card he selected is not amongst them, thus leaving him, and also the audience, to infer that the card taken from the point of the sword was really the one selected and drawn.

To Make a Card Stand Upright on the Table

This is a simple little trick, and not of sufficient importance to be performed by itself. But in conjuring, it is necessary to introduce a certain amount of "by-play," more especially if you should happen to have amongst your audience one who seemed to consider that everything that you did was very simple, and said, as many persons will frequently do, "that he can do this or that himself." Get such a person to step forward, apparently to shuffle or draw a card for you, and when he has drawn one, ask him to stand it on the table. No doubt he will look at you, and if he does try to do so, the card will most naturally fall flat. Now tell him that he does not go the right way about it, and, taking the card from him, place it carefully on the table, where to his astonishment it will remain standing upright. The secret of this is that you use a small and simple piece of apparatus, in fact a strip of tin or brass, about an inch and a half in length, and half an inch in width, bent very slightly to the bottom of the interior surface. Have a small piece of lead soldered about an eighth of an inch thick, and about three-quarters of an inch in length. On the outer surface of the tin or brass plate have spread a thin layer of beeswax. You have this concealed in your hand, and in the act of placing the card on the table you slip this apparatus behind the card, nipping the card at the bottom, apparently to steady it, but in reality to cause the card to adhere to the waxed side. The weight of the lead on the other side acts as a counterpoise, thus allowing the card to stand upright. The wax will not leave any mark on the card, and the slip can be removed in the act of lifting the card from the table.

The Mechanical Card Box

This apparatus is used for changing one card to another. It is an oblong box, measuring about four and a half inches by three and a half, and four inches high. The box is so arranged internally that the front of the box without the lid is exactly the same area as the bottom of the box. Against the front lies a small slab of tin or zinc, working on a cloth hinge (as shown in fig. 27) at the lower edge, so that when released from the front it falls to the bottom (which it exactly covers). This flap and the whole interior of the box must

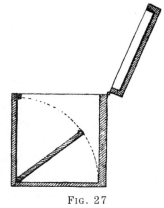

FIG. 27

be painted black. A little stud is fixed in the upper part of the flap, which, when closed against the front, fits into a little hole prepared for it in the lock, across which passes the tail of the bolt. When the key is turned as if locking the box (which, however, should be held open), the bolt of the lock is pushed forward and, the flap being lifted up against the front, the stud passes into the little hole previously mentioned. When you turn the key again as if unlocking the box, the tail of the bolt will catch the stud and secure the flap. The box can then be examined without fear of the flap being discovered. As soon as it is closed and the key turned to lock it, the bolt, being again shot forward, releases the stud, and the flap falls. When in use, place a card upon the flap (say the ace of hearts), and it is then folded and secured as above to the front of the box. The box is then shown empty, and the card to be changed (say the ten of diamonds) is placed at the bottom of the box, and you request some person to lock the box. The trick proceeds, and when this person again unlocks the box, to his surprise he finds the card changed to the ace of hearts. Many interesting tricks with small hand-kerchiefs can also be performed with this particular box.

The Card and Bird Box

This box is very similar to that last described (having a space below the flap); but its working is different, as in this box the flap has to lie folded against the back of the box, where it is fastened by means of a small spring. It can, however, be folded down to lie parallel with the bottom, a small catch pro-jecting from the inner surface of the front keeping it in that

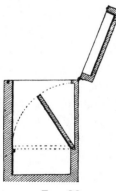

position, as shown in fig. 28. In this case the lock is only a sham, having neither key nor keyhole, but a small stud projecting from the lower edge of the lid, and representing the "sta-ple" of the lock; this presses, when you close the box, upon an upright pin passing up the front, through the thickness of the wood, thus withdrawing the catch when the flap flies up, concealing the card which was or has been placed upon it, and revealing a small bird, or any small article, which was previously concealed beneath it. Many interesting tricks can be performed with this box.

FIG. 28

Mechanical Cards

All cards of this description have the same object, the apparent transformation of a card to a different one—for

example, to change a king of spades to a
king of hearts. This is effected by having the
card made double, the pips at the corners
undergoing an alteration. This can better be
understood by looking at figs. 29, 30, 31.

Another form of changing card is the "flap
card." This is a card across whose center is
fixed a movable flap of exactly half its size.
When the flap is folded one way it covers the
upper half, and when folded down the other
way, it reveals a different surface (see fig.
32).

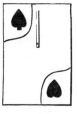

FIG. 30

Such mechanical cards, and many other
kinds, are to be bought at any conjuring
shop. These cards are used in various ways,
according to the fancy of the performer.

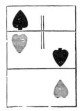

The Spelling-Bee Trick

This trick is a very interesting one, and one
in which no sleight of hand is required. The
method of working the trick is as follows:

FIG. 31

The performer selects from a pack
of cards thirteen, each one different,
for example the ace, two, three, four,
five, six, seven, eight, nine, ten, knave,
queen, and king. It does not matter
which suit the cards are taken from, or
whether the number is selected and
made up from the four suits, as long as
the cards have the required number of

FIG. 32

pips upon them. The performer takes the cards and lays them in a row upon the table in the order given above, and then, apparently picking up a card here and there, to get them well mixed instead of shuffling them, he proceeds to show the cards to his audience to prove that they are well mixed. The performer now informs his audience that he will attempt the difficult feat of spelling out all the cards one by one, and in the regular order as they were originally placed upon the table. Taking the first card, he says *O*, and passes that card to the bottom; he next takes the second card and says *N*, and passes that to the bottom; and taking the third card he says *E*, and passes that also to the bottom; then, taking the fourth card, he exhibits it, when it will be found to be the one, or ace, and he places that card, which he has spelled, upon the table. The performer next repeats the same, only this time spelling the word *t-w-o*, and so on through the pack until he comes to the knave, being always careful to place the card spelled upon the table, and not retain it in his hand. When the performer comes to the knave, he addresses his audience, and says that he holds only three cards in his hand, and he has to spell two out of three, and he then commences the same performance as before, spelling the word k-n-a-v-e, and taking the top card each time he names a letter and passing it to the bottom, and after spelling the word takes off the top card and exhibits the knave.

Now the performer is left with only two cards to spell the word *q-u-e-e-n;* but he repeats the same as before, passing the top card to the bottom each time he names a letter until the word is spelled, when he exhibits the top card, which is the queen, at the same time addressing his audience, and saying, that he has spelled twelve out of the thirteen cards, and there being only one card left, the king, it is impossible to spell that, but exhibiting it at the same moment. If the performer works this trick quickly, it cannot fail to elicit applause, appearing marvelous to the audience.

As we stated before, it does not depend upon the skill of the performer in using sleight of hand, as the real secret of the trick is knowing the order in which to pick up and place the cards. When the performer has laid the cards in regular order upon the table, he apparently picks a card up here and there indiscriminately, but in reality he takes the cards up in the following order: three, eight, seven, ace, king, six, four, two, queen, knave, ten, nine, and five, picking up the cards with the right hand, and placing them in the palm of the left, *face upward*, until he has picked up all the cards. He then reverses the position, bringing them backs uppermost, and commences to spell each card out in its regular order until he has spelled the twelve cards.

A very little practice will make the student thoroughly proficient with this trick; the main thing, however, is that the student shall have a good memory to remember the exact order in which the cards are to be picked up, because one slight error will spoil the whole trick.

The Three-Card Trick

This trick is sometimes practiced on the unwary, and many foolish persons have lost money through betting with unscrupulous persons in railway carriages, upon race-

FIG. 33

courses, and even in public places of resort. However, it is not with the idea of teaching my readers to cheat their friends, but to amuse them, that I explain this trick, which is extremely simple and easily performed. The performer exhibits three cards; for example the ace, two, and three of hearts, and he places them upon the table, showing each card as he does so, and then asks his friends to tell him where he placed the ace. They will of course point to the card that they took for the ace, and the performer, picking it up quickly, exhibits it—when to the surprise of the audience it will appear to be the three of hearts.

This can be repeated as often as the performer likes, he showing the ace each time, yet after he has laid it face downward upon the table, it will appear to be changed into the three when he picks it up. The secret of this is that the supposed ace card has two spots, or pips, upon it, as shown in fig. 33, and the performer in showing the cards keeps his thumb over the lower pip until he places it upon the table; but when he picks it up, instead of taking the card by the bottom as before, he picks it up by the top end, keeping his thumb over the blank space, when it appears as if the card has really changed to the three. The audience, seeing the two pips, naturally concludes that there is another pip beneath his finger or thumb. The performer must be careful, however, not to give the cards out to be examined, otherwise the deception would be at once discovered.

The Card Table

This ingenious piece of apparatus is of great use in many card tricks. It is a small table, or pedestal, standing about four inches in height, with a flat but round top. This top is blacked. Over this again is a false top made to fit it exactly, and blacked also; and it cannot be seen, even at very close quarters, that the little table has a false top.

Over this again a brass dome-shaped cover fits, which, if pressed down tightly over the table, will, when it is lifted up, bring with it the false top of the little table. There are many methods of using the table, but the following is the most universal *modus operandi.*

The performer brings forward the small table (with the false top on) and exhibits it to his audience, showing them that it is perfectly plain, and that it is impossible to conceal the smallest thing on it. Placing this upon the table, he takes forward a pack of cards and requests some person to draw a card, contriving, however, to force the required card, and taking care to have a similar card concealed under the false top of the small table. Replace the pack upon the table, and ask for the drawn card, which you immediately tear in pieces; then place it carefully upon the false top of the small table, taking care not to drop any of the pieces. Now exhibit the brass cover, to show that there is nothing whatever concealed within it. Placing it over the small table, press it down sharply, and it will nip the false top. Wave your wand and say, "One, two, three! Card be restored!" Upon lifting the cover, the concealed card is brought to view, thus appearing to the audience to be restored to its former condition. Fig. 34 will give the student a fair idea of the table in all its parts: "1" being the table proper, "2" the false top, and "3" the brass cover.

In concluding my remarks upon cards, I might state that there are many other tricks with cards, but to describe them all would make a work in itself. If the student can thoroughly make himself master of all these tricks that I have been describing, he will do well.

FIG. 34

CHAPTER 4

TRICKS WITH COINS

To Make a Quarter and a Penny Change Places

Borrow a quarter and a penny, getting the owners to mark them. Borrow two pocket handkerchiefs, and have palmed in your left hand a penny of your own; take the borrowed coins in your right hand, and apparently transfer them to your left, but only transfer the quarter, retaining the marked penny in your right palm. Show the audience the quarter and penny you have in your left hand, and place them on your table.

Now take up one of the borrowed handkerchiefs, and picking up the quarter, apparently place it in the handkerchief, but in reality place therein the marked penny you had in your hand. Request some person to hold this handkerchief tightly below the coin and well above his head. Now take the other penny (which is your own) from the table and apparently wrap it, in like manner, in the other handkerchief, but in reality substitute the quarter which was in your palm. Drop the substitute penny secretly into your *pochette*. Give the second handkerchief to another person to hold, and inform the audience that you will now make the coins change places. Get the two persons to advance toward each other, and rap each handkerchief with your wand, at the same time saying, "Change!" When they open the handkerchiefs, the coins will appear to have really changed places.

To Pass Two Marked Coins Wrapped in Separate Handkerchiefs into One Handkerchief

For this illusion the coins used in the preceding trick will suffice. You will also require two handkerchiefs, in the center of one of which you must have a penny stitched. Now take the prepared handkerchief, and pretend to place the marked penny therein, but retain this coin in the center of your palm, and hand the handkerchief to some person to hold, just below the coin. Next take your other handkerchief and, showing the quarter, place it in the center of the handkerchief, at the same time slipping the marked penny in also; take the handkerchief just below the coins, giving it a slight twist to prevent them from chinking against each other, and hand this also to another person to hold.

Now take your wand, and, informing your audience that you will pass the penny invisibly from the other handkerchief and cause it to appear in company with the quarter, slightly rap the handkerchief containing the supposed penny, saying the word "Pass," and request the person holding that handkerchief to take it by the corner and shake it, upon which it will appear as if the penny has really passed from it; now, taking a plate in your right hand, request the person holding the other handkerchief to shake the contents onto the plate. Both marked coins will drop onto the plate, much to his surprise.

To Pass a Marked Penny into the Center of an Orange

For this experiment you must get a piece of glass, cut round, and exactly the same size as a penny, which you must have palmed in your right hand. Have placed on the back of your table an orange, with a slit cut in it penetrating into the center, and have in readiness a small glass tumbler filled with water. Having this all prepared, ask your audience to lend you a penny, but to be sure to mark it. When this is handed to you, request some person to come forward. Hand him the penny, asking him to examine it well, so that he will be sure to know it again. While he is doing so, borrow a pocket handkerchief, and then bring on the tumbler of water, which you must ask the person on the stage to hold in his left hand. Taking the penny from him, you apparently place it in the handkerchief, but in reality substitute for it the piece of glass.

Now request the person to hold the penny by the edges, through the handkerchief, and to hold it just above the glass of water, letting the handkerchief fall around it. While he is holding the supposed penny, step quickly toward your table and, picking the orange up, slip the marked penny from your palm into the slit, and bring it forward, and show your audience, and tell them you will endeavour to pass the penny from the glass, and through the handkerchief, into the orange.

Replace the orange upon your table, but this time at the front part, and request the person to let go the penny piece he is holding, when you count "three." At that word he must drop it, and as it falls to the bottom of the glass the audience can hear the sound of its falling.

Draw their attention to this, and taking your wand in your right hand, touch the glass through the handkerchief, saying, "Pass," at the same time taking the handkerchief from off the glass of water, when it will appear as if the penny had gone, because the piece of glass, being transparent, cannot be seen at the bottom of the water.

Place the glass of water on the table and, taking the orange in your left hand and a knife in your right, bring it forward at the same time, putting the knife sharply into the slit. Appear to have changed your mind about cutting it yourself, and hand it to the person on the stage to cut, which, when he has done so, greatly to his surprise, will show the marked penny embedded in the center of the orange.

Hand the penny back to the owner, and ask if he is satisfied that it is the same coin, which, of course, he will be.

This is one of the best illusions with coins, and always astonishes beholders if done neatly.

The Multiplied Coins

This is a very good illusion if care is taken in performing it. Palm three pennies in your left hand, and with the same hand take up a small plate, the coins being under the plate. Next borrow twelve pennies from your audience, and request some gentleman to count them out; then borrow a gentleman's hat, and get a person to hold it, and pour the twelve coins from the plate into the hat, at the same time letting fall the three you had concealed in your palm. You now ask him how many coins he has in the hat, and having counted them before, he will naturally say twelve; tell him to take out three coins and hand them to you, and ask him how many remain, and he will say nine.

Walk to your table, and take the coins into your left hand, and apparently place them in your right, but in reality palm them in your left hand, and then with the left hand take up your wand, and touch your right hand, at the same time commanding the coins to fly from your hand to the hat. Open your right hand, and to the audience they will appear to have gone. Secretly drop the three coins from your left hand into your *pochette* or *profonde.* Now ask the gentleman holding the hat to turn the coins out on to the plate. When he has done so, and counts them, to his surprise there will be twelve pennies.

To Pass Three Coins into a Tumbler

For this experiment, have ready a glass tumbler with three pennies in it on your *servante,* and have another tumbler standing on your table. At the back of your curtain, your assistant must be in readiness with a tumbler and three pennies.

Having all in readiness, commence by borrowing three pennies, and place them on a plate upon your table. Now bring forward the empty tumbler and a cardboard cover made to fit over it. Allow the audience to examine them, and when they are returned to you, take them to the table, but in passing them back, quickly exchange the tumblers, placing the empty one on the *servante* and the one containing the three coins on the table, and place over it the cardboard cover.

Now take the three borrowed coins from the plate with your left hand, and apparently put them into your right, but in reality palm them. Close your right hand, take your wand into your left, and, sharply touching your right hand with it, command the coins to pass one by one into the glass tumbler. As you say, "One, two, three," your assistant drops a coin into the tumbler at the back of the curtain at each word. Your audience will imagine that they have really passed into the tumbler, as they can hear the sound of each coin dropping into a glass.

Lift the cover and show the coins in the glass, and, taking the plate with your right hand and the glass in your left, apparently pour out the coins into the plate, but in reality only drop the three coins you have palmed, preventing the other three from dropping from the glass, which you now place at the back of your table, or pour out, unseen to the audience, into the box of sawdust on your *servante*. Take the plate forward and hand the coins back to their respective owners, getting them to examine them, to see that they are the same they marked and gave you.

To Change a Quarter into a Penny

This is a very simple trick but, if cleverly performed, will no doubt puzzle many. For this illusion, get two large sheets of thick white writing paper; cut out four square pieces and fold each piece over the same way, and exactly the same size; take two of them and carefully glue the backs together, and do the same with the other pieces. Now take a quarter of your own and place it in one side of the folded papers, laying this with the coin downward on one corner of your table; now take the other paper and place a penny in one of the folds, and place this coin downward on the other corner of your table.

Having this all in readiness, step forward and request some person or persons to lend you a quarter and a penny, and to be sure to mark them. Take the paper in your left hand, already containing the penny of your own, place the quarter in the other or upper fold, letting the audience see you do so; now place it back on your table, but reverse the positions, this time bringing the penny uppermost. Walk to the other corner of your table and, taking the other paper as you did at first, place the marked penny in the upper fold, and reverse this also in replacing it on your table, bringing your quarter uppermost. Now take your wand and inform your audience that by merely touching each paper with your wand, you will cause each coin to change place. Touch each paper with your wand and, picking up the one in which you placed the quarter, take out the penny (which is your own), replace it in the paper, and place it again on the table, but this time bringing the quarter uppermost; take the other paper, and show the quarter, thus causing the audience to believe that they really have changed places. Replace this paper on your table, reversing it, and bringing the marked penny uppermost, and tell your audience that you will now endeavor to execute a more difficult feat—to cause the coins to go back to their original respective positions.

Taking your wand, again repeat the same as at first, and of course, upon opening each paper, the coins will appear to have gone back to their original places. Hand the marked coins to their respective owners, and place the papers on the back of your table out of the observation of the audience. Care must be taken, in doing this simple trick, not to allow the audience to get sight of the underneath part of the papers; otherwise they would at once know they were double. A little practice will make the student sufficiently expert to prevent this from occurring.

The Flying Coins and Handkerchief

This is a capital trick, and the apparatus can be made by the student at a small and trifling expense. Get a stout sheet of cardboard and cut out a piece eight inches long by four inches wide. Next cut out two pieces to form the sides, and then two small ends, but leave the top open; have it made about two and a half or three inches in height. Now make a small drawer to fit into this box, with two compartments, glueing on the top end; next fix a quarter of a cover to fit over each end, thus leaving an opening in the center, but be sure these covers are exactly the same size as each of the compartments in the small drawer, as shown in fig. 35. Now

FIG. 35

place in box number 2 a white handkerchief, keeping it well under one of the half-covers. Provide yourself with a handkerchief similar to the one thus concealed. In the palm of your left hand, conceal and palm three quarters; having all this in readiness, have your assistant placed behind your curtain with a glass and three coins, ready to drop in at the signal from you.

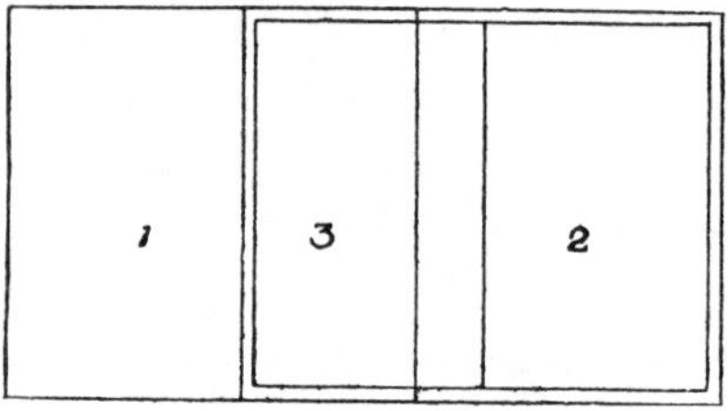

Now commence by borrowing from your audience three quarters and requesting each person to mark them. While this is being done, take the handkerchief from your table and place it across your left hand, having the palmed coins underneath. Collect the marked coins in a plate and, placing the plate on your table, apparently take them off the plate and place them in the handkerchief, but in reality slip in the coins you had palmed, taking care to palm the three marked coins in their stead in your left hand. Now pick up your wand and place it in your left hand, thus preventing the audience from seeing that you hold anything else in that hand. Get some person to hold the handkerchief, and to satisfy himself that the coins are really in it. Now take an empty tumbler, which you show to your audience, and place it at the back of your table. Take the handkerchief from the person holding it, and roll it up, placing it in drawer number 3.

Now show the audience the back of the box, and thus satisfy them that it has not a false back; this will give you the opportunity of sliding compartment number 2 under cover number 1, leaving exposed the handkerchief placed there first, and which contains no coins, but this the audience will believe to be the one with the coins in it. Taking this handkerchief out very carefully, as if to prevent the coins from dropping out, place it upon your table.

Now borrow a gentleman's hat and place it over the handkerchief, and next taking the tumbler in your left hand, request some gentleman to lend you a handkerchief, and as you place it over the tumbler, slip the palmed coins into it, taking care to do it very carefully, so as not to attract the attention of your audience. Place the glass thus covered over with the handkerchief upon your table and, taking up your wand, command the coins to pass one by one from the handkerchief covered by the hat, into the glass tumbler covered with the other handkerchief. Touch the hat with your wand, saying, "Pass one," "two," "three," and your assistant will at each word drop a coin into the glass he has behind the curtain, thus leading the audience to believe that the sound they heard was really that of the coins dropping one by one into the covered glass. Request some person to remove the handkerchief from the glass, when he will discover the three marked quarters, and upon removing the hat and shaking the handkerchief that had been placed beneath, he will really believe that they have left the handkerchief. With a little practice, this cannot fail to cause a sensation amongst your audience.

To Cause a Coin to Leave a Handkerchief
and Pass into an Orange Covered with a Glass

Have ready on your table an orange with a slit cut in it, and also a glass tumbler beside it. Next place a penny on your table, and on one side put a little soft beeswax; have this ready on your table beside a small plate. Commence by borrowing a pocket handkerchief, which is spread out on your table. Take up the plate, and at the same time the penny already prepared. Ask some person to lend you a penny, and to mark it, and place it on the plate, handing him the plate at the same time for him to do so. When he returns it to you, and as you are walking toward your table to lay the plate down, exchange quickly the pennies, placing the waxed one on the plate. Pick this one up and place it in the center of the borrowed handkerchief, pressing it very hard at the same time, wax side downward, thus causing it to stick to the handkerchief. Fold the corners over it, and knock it on the table, that the audience may hear it is there.

Now bring forward the orange, taking care, however, at the same time to slip the marked penny into the slit. Show this to your audience, and place it on the plate, covering it with the glass tumbler.

Now pick up the handkerchief, giving it a knock at the same time on your table, so that the audience may hear it is there; and inform them that you will command the penny to leave the handkerchief and pass into the orange. Take the handkerchief by the corners, and, saying "Pass," shake it slightly, but taking care to keep the coin toward your chest, when it will seem to have disappeared. Draw the handkerchief through your hand carefully, at the same time detaching the coin, which secretly drop into your *pochette*.

Now lift the glass and, bringing the plate forward, request some person to cut open the orange, but slip the point of the knife (as if accidentally) into the slit in the orange yourself. Of course, when the orange is cut, to the astonishment of all, the marked penny is discovered.

The Multiplying Money Plate

This is a specially prepared piece of apparatus, although in appearance it seems an ordinary china plate. This plate is made with a false bottom, having a narrow flat space running across the center of the under surface of the plate, but of course concealed by the false bottom. This space is made large enough to conceal a row of coins (either pennies, nickels, or quarters, as the case may be). This is closed at one end but open at the other, to allow the coins to slide out, as shown in fig. 36.

Place in this hollow space as many coins as it will hold (say four pennies), and, holding the plate with the opening toward your hand, request some person to place, say, twelve pennies on the plate, and to count them; he will of course count only twelve. Now ask him for the loan of his

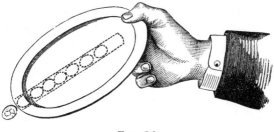

F<small>IG</small>. 36

hat, and at the same time, turning the plate around, empty the contents into the hat, and the four concealed coins will of course drop into the hat with the other twelve placed on the plate. You can now work this trick in the same manner as the trick described before, "The Multiplied Coins," only taking care to take the same number of coins out of the hat as you had concealed in the hollow space beneath the plate.

The Rattling Coin Box

This is a small box measuring about three inches by two inches, and one inch in depth externally, but internally it is only about half that depth, and the end piece of the slide lid is of such depth as to be flush with the bottom. Therefore, if a coin is placed in this box, and the box is held slanting downward, and the lid slightly open, as in fig. 37, the coin will slide down into the performer's hand holding the box. Between the true and false bottom is placed a small piece of copper or zinc, and if the box is shaken laterally, this will rattle. In its normal condition, however, this piece of metal is held fast by the action of a small spring placed between the two bottoms, but which can be released by pressure on

FIG. 37

the bottom of the box. Showing this box, the performer borrows a marked coin, which is placed in the box, and which he immediately gets into his possession as described above, and palms it, closing the box and passing it to his other hand. Shaking the box causes the copper or zinc to rattle, thus leading the audience to believe it is the coin they hear.

Placing the box on his table, the performer gets rid of the marked coin by passing it secretly into any other piece of apparatus he thinks fit. Having done so, he now commands the coin to leave the box, which he shakes, but this time pressing the spring so it remains silent, and opening the box it is found empty: afterwards the borrowed coin is produced from elsewhere, as arranged beforehand by the performer.

The Pepper Box

This is another piece of apparatus for making pennies or quarters vanish, and can be used in the course of any trick where it is necessary to get possession of the borrowed and marked coin. This box, to all appearance, is precisely the same as a large pepper box, as shown in fig. 38. The box portion is made double, consisting of two tubes sliding one in the other, the bottom

FIG. 38

FIG. 39

being soldered to the inner one. By pulling the bottom slightly down you draw down the inner tube, and bring into view a small slit at one side of the inner tube, just level with the bottom, and of a sufficient size to allow a quarter to pass easily through, as shown in fig. 39. The lid is specially prepared, having an inner or false top, and between the true and false top a loose piece of metal is introduced, which rattles when the box is shaken; but if you wish it to remain silent, then press down a little point of wire projecting from one of the holes at the top. This box is usually enameled black, and can be had at any conjuring shop.

The Plug Box

This is a very ingenious piece of apparatus, and no performer should be without it. It is made of brass, and is about three inches in height and one and a half inches in diameter, and is composed of four

FIG. 40

separate parts. In fig. 40, *A* represents the outside of the box, being a brass tube open at both ends with a movable bottom, *B*, which fits tightly into the lower end of *A*, being apparently a fixture, and thus forming a complete whole. The tube *A* has no lid, but is closed by inserting what appears to be a solid brass plug; but this plug, though apparently solid, is composed of two parts—the plug, C, which is solid, and a brass sheath D, fitting over C exactly, but about a quarter of an inch longer, thus leaving, when you place C in D, and push it well down, a hollow space at the bottom of D capable of containing a quarter.

The sheath D is exactly the same length as A, and will fit easily upon C, but tightly within A. When the plug box is shown to the audience, the bottom B is in its proper place, and C, which, shown apart from A, is covered with its sheath or cover. The audience will naturally conclude that the apparatus consists of two parts only. If you now place the plug in the box, and push it well down, the bottom B will be pushed out and fall into the performer's hand. On withdrawing the plug, the sheath D is left within A; the bottom of D, which comes flush with the lower edge of A, appears now to be the bottom of the latter.

To the audience the box appears to be exactly the same as when first shown, and can be handed around for examination.

The plug box can be used to produce, reproduce, or exchange.

The best mode of using the plug box is as follows:

Take a quarter and wrap it in a small piece of paper; press it well to retain the shape, and then take out the coin, again folding the paper, which will appear to still contain the coin. Place the paper thus prepared in D, and the performer, borrowing a quarter, requests the person to wrap it in a piece of paper of the same size and similar in appearance to the other.

The quarter now wrapped up is placed in A, and the box closed, the performer thus getting possession of the coin and paper. Now hand the box to the owner of the quarter and ask him to see if his money is still there, and seeing the folded paper at the bottom, which appears to be the same, he answers in the affirmative. Now close the box and you can dispose of the coin according to your own fancy. Handing the owner the box again, ask him to take his money out and open the paper; he will imagine his money has flown away, leaving the paper behind. The borrowed coin can now be produced from any source the performer fancies, or if he is expert he can apparently take it from the beard or hat of the person to whom the quarter belonged.

The Magic Cabinet

This piece of apparatus is not only used for obtaining possession of coins, but also of rings, watches, etc. It is a small cabinet about four inches high and two and a half inches square, and consists of two parts: an outer case, covered at top, but open otherwise throughout, and a small drawer (as shown in fig. 41). This cabinet has no bottom, and when the drawer is out, it can be handed for examination. At the back

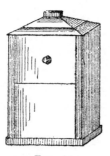

Fig. 41

of the cabinet is a small brass pin projecting from the back on the inside, just on a level with the bottom of the drawer. In the back of the drawer is a small hole into which the brass pin fits, and the pressure of this pin, when the drawer is placed in the cabinet, releases a small catch, and allows the bottom of the drawer to fall (as shown in fig. 42), thus allowing any article placed in the

drawer to fall into the hand of the performer holding the cabinet, as shown in
fig. 43. In pulling the drawer out again,
the bottom of it again resumes its
proper position, fastening itself by the
mere action of pulling it out of the cabinet.

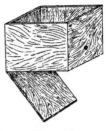

FIG. 42

We now suppose the performer has
obtained possession of the coin or article
placed in the drawer, and taking the top of
the cabinet with his other hand, he carefully places it in front of his table, in the
full view of his audience, meanwhile palming the borrowed article. He can now conclude the trick by reproducing it in any
manner he may think proper, of course
handing the cabinet to the person who
placed the article in it, to show that it has really left it.

FIG. 43

The Miraculous Money Casket

This is a neat velvet- or leather-covered box, three inches by
two, and two and a half inches high. Inside it is lined with a
velvet cushion, with four small slits, just large enough to
hold a quarter as shown in fig. 44. This is fitted inside with
a mechanical arrangement, so contrived that each time you
close the box, one of the coins drops through into a lower
chamber, or false bottom, until all the coins have vanished.
Having procured this casket, you place it on your table in
readiness; your assistant being behind the curtain, to be
ready at your signal, with a glass and four coins.

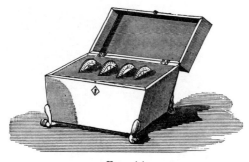

Fig. 44

Now place on the back of your table a glass tumbler, and in your right hand have palmed four quarters and step forward and request your audience to lend you four coins (similar to those you have palmed), and after being duly marked, receive them all into your left hand, and making the pass, apparently transfer them to your right, but in reality palm them in your left.

Now place the four coins one by one into the casket, from your *right* hand, and, closing it, request some person to hold it. Taking a pocket handkerchief in your left hand, show with your right hand the empty glass; but in placing it on the table and covering it with the handkerchief, secretly and quietly slip in the four marked coins. Walking forward, you now tell your audience that you will command the coins to leave the casket one by one, and pass into the glass upon the table. The gentleman holding the box opens it to see the coins are all there, and closing it again, you say "One." Your assistant, at the word, drops a coin into the glass he holds behind the curtain. The person is requested to open the casket, which he does, and he finds one coin gone. It is again closed, and the same operation is repeated until all the coins have disappeared, your assistant dropping a coin at each word, when you call, "Two, three, four." The casket is then opened and found to be empty, and being returned is placed on the table, and the glass is brought forward, and the coins, being poured out, are found upon examination to be those that had been marked.

In connection with this trick there is a more elaborate piece of apparatus, called the "Crystal Cash Box," which is described hereafter, under the heading of "Stage Tricks and Illusions" (chapter 10), and which many performers use for producing the borrowed coins. But the above is the simplest and least expensive mode for the beginner, the casket being the only article that would have to be bought.

The Vanishing Plate

This piece of apparatus can be better understood by referring to the diagram given in fig. 45. A number of coins placed upon the plate (which is made of metal) are caused to disappear one by one in the act of counting them, this disappearance being caused by slightly pressing the center

FIG. 45

of the plate, which causes the center portion to fall a little to one side, allowing the coins to slide under the rim and fall into a hollow space beneath.

The Tray of Proteus

This salver or tray is somewhat similar to the contrivance just described, but it is so constructed that it will add, subtract, or cause to vanish coins that are placed upon it under the very eyes of the audience. It is divided in the center, as shown in fig. 46, and one half is movable. The opposite or fixed side is divided lengthwise into two platforms. Coins can be placed in these partitions, and in such case would multiply the coins placed on the salver, as by pressing down the movable side of the tray, and holding the fixed end slanting upward, it would allow the concealed coins to slide out on the movable portion of the tray. If required for causing coins to vanish, the movable side would have to be pressed down and the tray slanted slightly downward, which would cause the coins to slide under the fixed half of the

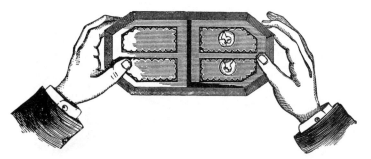

Fig. 46

tray, and when the pressure is released, the tray would appear empty. Beneath the tray is a small slide, to allow any money concealed in the interior of the tray to fall through, if necessary.

To Pass a Penny into a Corked Bottle

This is a most ingenious piece of apparatus, which forms a very brilliant illusion, and can be used in the working of many tricks with coins. The principal piece of apparatus is ingeniously constructed, yet to all appearance is only an ordinary cork. However, the inside of this cork has been cleanly cut out, and a brass chamber is fitted within the hollow, with a round disc of brass working up and down, and kept in position, or released, by means of a small brass catch projecting through the cork and near the top. The arrangement and mechanism can be understood by referring to the diagrams shown in fig. 47, in which A represents the outside of the cork and B a small brass catch which releases the disc of metal C working up and down the cen-

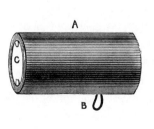
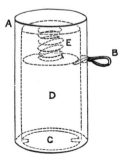

FIG. 47

ter, and when released forced to the bottom of the brass inner barrel D by means of a spiral spring E. At the bottom of the inner barrel are two small catches or lips of brass, to prevent the disc C from being forced right out. The performer provides himself with a plain cork, in appearance the same as the mechanical one. The coin to be used for this trick is a penny cut across in three pieces and secured together by means of a small rubber band, or watch spring, and this coin can be folded over into three, and in that condition is forced up the inside of the mechanical cork, and there it remains until ejected by means of the little brass catch B.

There are many methods in which this piece of apparatus can be used; the following, however, is the one usually adopted by the author.

The performer, having borrowed a marked penny, places it in a small box and locks it, the key being taken possession of by the owner of the coin. The box is then placed upon the front of the table, in full view of the audience, and the performer now brings forward a glass bottle and a cork, and, exhibiting them to his audience, he places the cork in the neck of the bottle, and informs them that at his command the coin will fly from the box into the interior of the bottle, notwithstanding that the bottle is well corked. Standing well in front of his audience, the performer holds the bottle by the neck and slowly counts "One, two, three," and at the same moment he releases the spring catch, and the coin is seen and heard to fall inside the bottle, which is shown to the audience to satisfy them that the penny is really there. Walking to the table, the performer quickly substitutes the genuine cork for the mechanical cork, and brings forward the box and the bottle.

The box is handed to the person who has possession of the key, and he is then requested to unlock it. He does so and finds it empty. The box is then replaced, and the performer, taking the bottle, holds it upside down, and by giving it a sharp downward shake the penny falls into the hand of the performer. He exhibits the coin, but does *not* hand it for examination. He hands the bottle and cork to be examined by any person in the audience, to show that there is nothing mechanical about them. Now, turning toward his table, the performer directs the attention of his audience either to an orange or to some special piece of apparatus, and takes the coin. He makes the pass to take it from left to right, but palming it in the left hand, and holding the right hand in the attitude of throwing, he says, "One, two, three," and opens his right hand. The coin is seen to have vanished, and upon picking up the orange or piece of apparatus that was selected, the marked penny is found within it, having been, of course, placed there previously by the performer in one of his journeys to the table. There are many other methods of performing, but this particular one, as described, if worked neatly and quickly, will please any audience.

CHAPTER 5

TRICKS WITH RINGS

The Vanishing Ring

The performer, in exhibiting any tricks with rings, should always choose wedding rings, for as these are made plain, it is a very simple matter to provide a substitute or dummy ring; indeed, he would do well to have always to hand several cheap gilt wedding rings. The vanishing ring is a very simple contrivance, and can always be used to advantage in performing most of the tricks with rings. To a common gilt wedding ring, attach a small piece of fine white silk, and attach the other end of this silk to a piece of fine cord elastic, fastened to the inside of the performer's coat, and brought down the left sleeve in such a manner that when the arm hangs by the side the ring falls within a couple of inches of the edge of the cuff. Thus, taking the ring between the finger and thumb will cause the elastic to stretch, and upon releasing the ring it will instantly fly up the coat sleeve. This ring can be used, as I stated before, in nearly every case when the performer is doing ring tricks.

One method is to borrow a lady's wedding ring. Receiving it in your right hand, you make the pass, as if transferring it to your left, but palming it in your right; have the substitute ring ready in your left, which you instantly show. Now take a piece of paper, place it on your table, and pretend to wrap in it the ring used as a substitute for the borrowed ring. Pressing the paper tightly will cause it to retain the impression of the ring; in making the last fold, however, release the ring, which will fly up your sleeve. Fold the paper as if the ring were still contained in it, and place it in sight of the audience.

Having obtained possession of the real ring, you can produce it in any way you think fit, from any other piece of apparatus—from an orange, egg, etc.—and having placed it ready, now command the ring to leave the paper and pass into whatever piece of apparatus you may select, and upon anyone in the audience opening the paper, the ring will be found to have disappeared, to be found elsewhere, as you may determine.

To Pass a Ring from One Hand onto Any Finger of the Other

This is another trick where the vanishing ring comes again into use. Have a small hook sewed to the side of your trousers, point upward, and just on a level with the fingers when the hand is dropped by the side. Having borrowed a ring, as described before, show the substitute in the left hand and let your right hand drop casually to your side, slipping the borrowed ring onto the hook. Now inform your audience that you will cause the ring to pass from your left hand onto any finger of your right they may select, at the same time waving the right hand to show there is nothing in it, after which again drop the right hand to your side. As soon as the finger is chosen, slip that finger into the borrowed ring, immediately closing your right hand, to conceal it. Then, holding your left hand out in front of you, say, "One, two, three! Pass!" and at once release the substitute ring, which will disappear. The left hand is then shown empty, while upon opening the right, the borrowed ring is discovered to have passed onto the finger selected.

The Suspended Ring

This is a very simple illusion, suitable for beginners. Soak in salt and water, for about five hours, about half a yard of common black thread, and when it is dry, tie one end to a ring, and the other end to the center of a walking stick. Place this stick across the backs of two chairs, letting the ring hang between, and now take a match, and set fire to the thread, which will be burnt to ashes, but the ring will not fall, but still remain suspended in the air.

To Pass a Ring from the Center of a Handkerchief into a Real Egg

For this trick, provide yourself with a large white handkerchief, from the center of which is suspended a common wedding ring by a short piece of white silk. Next get two wooden egg cups, but in the bottom of one have a small slot cut, capable of holding a ring in an upright position; have these on the back of your table, hidden by some bulky article or apparatus.

Now get a piece of stout wire, and bend it at one end to form a small hook; have on your table two or three eggs placed on a plate.

All being in readiness, borrow a wedding ring and request

some person to hold it, apparently placing it in the center of the handkerchief, but in reality palming it, substituting for it the suspended ring. Get the person to hold this suspended ring over a small tray, the sides of the handkerchief hanging down all around. Stepping to your table, slip the real ring into the slot in the prepared egg cup and, picking up the other one, show it to your audience; place this again on your table, but quickly substitute the prepared egg cup.

Now, drawing the attention of your audience to the eggs, tell them you will pass the ring into any egg they may select. When they have chosen one, hold it in your left hand, and your wand in your right, and tell the person holding the ring in the handkerchief to drop it at the word "three." Saying "One, two, three! Pass!" give the egg a sharp tap with your wand at the small end, which of course will crack it. The person holding the ring having dropped it, it will of course fall on the tray, its fall being distinctly heard. Tell your audience that the ring has now passed into the egg, and, placing the egg in the prepared egg cup, *with the cracked end downward*, step forward and, taking the handkerchief from the tray by two corners, shake it slightly, with the suspended ring *toward your body*, thus proving that the ring has left the handkerchief. Bring the egg cup forward and, breaking the top of the egg, insert the wire hook, and the ring will be apparently brought out of the center of the egg. The performer can no doubt see the utility of appearing to crack the egg *accidentally*, because the egg, when placed sharply down into the egg cup, causes the ring fixed into the slot at the bottom to penetrate the egg. This is a splendid trick if performed neatly.

To Pass a Ring Through a Table

For this trick you use the handkerchief with the suspended ring as in the last trick. After borrowing a ring and appearing to place it in the handkerchief, get the person from whom you have borrowed it, or one of the audience, to hold it as before. Now borrow a gentleman's hat and, taking it in the hand that holds the palmed ring, inform your audience that you will command the ring to leave the handkerchief, pass through your table, and fall into the hat placed below it. Show the inside of the hat empty, and in placing it below your table, let fall into it the palmed ring. Saying, "One, two, three! Pass!" as before, lift the handkerchief and shake it, showing it empty, and taking the hat up show it with the ring inside.

CHAPTER 6

TRICKS WITH HANDKERCHIEFS

The Vanishing Handkerchief

This is not really meant for a trick, but simply to create a little diversion amongst the audience. To the center of a handkerchief sew a piece of fine white elastic cord, and to this again attach a piece of string; pass this up your coat sleeve, and sew the string inside the sleeve of the other arm, the cord thus crossing your back. Have the cord of such a length in all that the handkerchief will be drawn up your sleeve within, say, three inches of the bottom.

Coming in front of your audience, you remark that it is very warm, and placing your hands behind you, as if taking your handkerchief from your tail pocket, you take the opportunity of pulling the handkerchief down into your hand, crumpling it up, so that the cord cannot be seen. Bringing your hand in front, you wipe your face and forehead, and after doing so straighten the arm slightly in front of you, releasing at the same time the handkerchief, which will to the amazement of the audience appear to vanish, but in reality flying up your coat sleeve with lightninglike rapidity. This can be repeated as often as the performer chooses, simply pulling it down each time as above.

Fɪɢ. 48

The Handkerchief That Cannot Be Tied

The performer borrows a large handkerchief—a silk hand-kerchief if possible—and, twisting it like a rope, professes to tie a knot, or a series of knots, but on pulling the hand-kerchief it comes out quite straight. To do this, the per-former, before he pulls the knot tight, slips in his left thumb just beneath the tie, as shown in fig. 48.

The Knotted Handkerchiefs

For this trick you require two silk handkerchiefs. Twisting them rope-fashion, request some person to tie them, holding the two ends for them to do so. After this has been tied, take it in your hand, apparently to tighten the knot, but in reality take one end and draw it sharply the reverse way, when it will draw the handkerchief in a straight line, forming a slip-knot of the other handkerchief. Request some person—a lady if possible—to breathe on the knots, and, taking the knotted part in your hand, give a slight pull to the other handkerchief and they will be perfectly straight and free from knots.

Many performers perform this trick by using six or more borrowed handkerchiefs, and requesting some person to tie them all together. As each one is tied, the performer, apparently drawing the knots tighter, pulls the knot into the required position each time until they are all done. Then, borrowing a gentleman's tall hat, he puts the handkerchiefs—which to the audience are all tied together—into the hat, but as he places them slowly in the hat with his left hand, he pulls them loose with his right hand, one by one, as they are placed in the hat, and as the knots have all been drawn into the required position, it is a very easy matter to draw them one by one from the loop which holds them. This method is very effective, as the audience sees a number of handkerchiefs tied together and placed in the hat.

The performer, taking the hat in his hand, then asks for a little music and shakes it gently, upon which the handkerchiefs will fall out of the hat, one by one, perfectly free from knots. The knot is the same kind that people usually make in tying a parcel or package, and is called by sailors a common reef knot.

The Rope and Handkerchief

Get a piece of rope about twenty feet long and, showing this to your audience, borrow a handkerchief and request some person to tie your wrists together with it. Have the rope now drawn through the arms, and desire the person to hold the two ends of the rope tightly, bringing the rope between the wrists, running over and under the handkerchief. The person holding the rope tightly, the performer pulls tightly against him, which brings the rope well down *between* the wrists. Slacken the rope slightly, and with the fingers of the right hand draw the rope *through* the handkerchief and slip the hand through the loop of rope thus drawn through. Then, by making a sudden and slight pull, the performer will be free from the rope, his hands still remaining tied as at first.

This trick must be well practiced before the student can do it neatly and rapidly.

The Demon Handkerchief

This handkerchief is used for causing the disappearance of such articles as a coin, a card, an egg, a watch, or any other article of moderate size.

It consists of *two* handkerchiefs of the same pattern, neatly stitched together all around the edges, but with a slit in one edge about four inches in length in the middle. The space between the handkerchiefs thus forms a pocket, the slit forming the opening. In shaking the handkerchief, always keep the side with the slit in toward your body. In placing any article in the center, you can thus allow it to fall inside, and upon shaking the handkerchief, the article seems to have disappeared. The article thus obtained can be produced in any way the performer may think proper in working the remaining portion of the trick.

No conjurer should be without one of the above; it is very simple to make, and he can prepare it himself. Colored handkerchiefs are the best to use in making it.

How to Exchange a Borrowed Handkerchief for a Substitute

Have ready a handkerchief as a substitute for that you wish to borrow, and similar to it, tucked up under your waistcoat, out of sight. Borrowing a handkerchief, receive it in your right hand. Turning sharply around to walk toward your table, rapidly tuck it up your waistcoat, on the right side, at the same time pulling down the substitute with the left hand, and quickly transferring it to your right. The change will have been executed by the time you reach your table. The handkerchief now obtained can be produced in a variety of ways according to the pleasure of the performer.

The Magic Plumes

This is a very pretty illusion, although simple, and a little practice will enable the student to perform it well. Purchase a number of large feathers, say about twenty. Take off your coat, and place along each arm ten plumes with the stems just low enough for you to take hold of. These feathers lie very close, and when your coat is on, you can move your arms freely, and the audience cannot detect that you have anything concealed up your sleeves. Borrow a large silk handkerchief and shake it well, and draw through your hand to show there is nothing in it. Now ask for a little lively music, and, taking the handkerchief, let it hang for a moment in front of you, hiding your arms and hands. At the same instant, catch hold of one of the stems of the concealed plumes, and, shaking the handkerchief, allow it to fall to the floor. Repeat this until you have produced all the feathers, which will appear to be a large heap when loosely placed together on the stage.

To Produce a Shower of Sweets from a Borrowed Handkerchief

The secret of this trick lies in using a small bag similar to that shown on the left in fig. 49, which is represented open, releasing the sweets contained in it; the other, on the right,

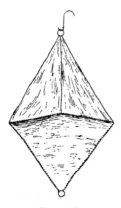

FIG. 49

represents the same bag when closed. Have this hanging from the top of the table at the back, which, of course, is hidden from the sight of the audience. The performer must also have a plate on the table. Borrowing a handkerchief, he walks to the back of the table and allows the hand holding the handkerchief to fall for a moment; in lifting it up again, he nips the hook shown in the diagram through the handkerchief and passes his other hand down the outside of the handkerchief, releasing at the same instant the flap of the little bag, thus allowing the sweets contained in it to fall apparently from the interior of the handkerchief onto the plate. After so doing, by holding the handkerchief over the *servante* and releasing the hook at the same moment, the concealed bag falls onto the hidden shelf. The handkerchief can be shaken and shown empty, and returned to its owner, and the sweets distributed amongst the juvenile portion of your audience, causing them a great amount of pleasure and satisfaction.

Some performers use two of these bags sewn back to back, thus causing a shower of two different kinds of sweets.

To Produce Any Number of Eggs from a Handkerchief

Obtain a large red handkerchief, and from from the center of the topmost edge suspend a hollowed-out egg attached to a piece of black thread or silk, allowing it to hang about halfway down. Place the egg in one corner, folding it up inside. Take the corner with the concealed egg in your left hand, and the opposite top corner in your right, and show the handkerchief to your audience, shaking it and showing it empty. Now borrow a tall hat and, placing it on one of your small tables, inform your audience you will show them a new way to lay eggs.

Holding the handkerchief across your chest, release the egg, which falls down at the back, being suspended by the thread, nip the center with your teeth just where the thread is attached to the edge of the handkerchief, and draw the two corners backward. Now hold the two top corners together with your right hand and the bottom corners with your left. Holding the handkerchief well up, allow your right to drop just over the hat, gently shaking the handkerchief, and the egg will fall into the hat, the audience not being able to see that this is attached to the handkerchief by the thread. While the egg is in the hat, show the two sides of the handkerchief empty and, taking the two top corners, allow it to hang down in front of the hat. Lifting it up again sud-

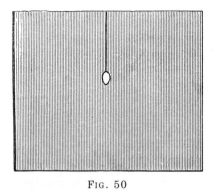

FIG. 50

denly of course brings the egg with it. This can be repeated any number of times, until the audience imagines the hat to be nearly full of eggs; then fold the handkerchief carelessly together, taking care to cover the suspended egg, and place it on your table. Take up the hat and, telling the audience you will make them a present of the eggs, pretend to throw the contents toward them. They will naturally duck their heads, expecting a shower of eggs; but to their surprise the eggs will appear to have vanished. This is a good illusion if performed quickly and neatly, but you must take care not to allow the concealed egg to be seen, except when in the act of falling into the hat. Fig. 50 will give the student a correct idea of the method of preparing this handkerchief.

CHAPTER 7

TRICKS WITH BALLS

The Cups-and-Ball Trick

This apparatus can be used to very great effect at times, but most of the performers of the present day discard it from their repertoire, and keep to more effective and amusing tricks. There are many sharpers of the present time, who are to be seen wherever a crowd is assembled, plying the above trick, only in a smaller form, under the name of the "pea and thimble" trick, inducing many persons to bet upon the position of the pea or small ball. The operation is so similar to that used by conjurers that I will describe it, and the reader can readily see how the poor victims are so easily duped. The accompanying illustrations given in figs. 51, 52, and 53 will also show the position of the hands in manipulating this apparently simple apparatus.

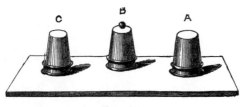

FIG. 51

The performer, having everything in readiness, takes the ball between his first finger and thumb and, while apparently conveying it under the cup A, dexterously uses his thumb, and places the ball between the second and third fingers, where it is clipped and held tight by the contraction of the fingers; at the same moment he lifts B, pretends to drop it, and, while picking it up, places the ball under the cup B. The onlooker fixes his eyes upon the latter and is surprised, when the cup C is lifted, to see the ball under it. The onlooker, of course, naturally concludes that all this parade is made to draw his attention off B. The various positions are shown in fig. 52, and of course the performer may so arrange that the ball is always concealed between his fingers, and if the three cups were lifted simultaneously, it would at once be seen that the ball is not under any of them. Thus with these tricksters, when using this apparatus, the unfortunate person is induced to bet upon the position of the ball, when in reality it is concealed in the hand of the performer, who can, by lifting one of the other cups, cause it to appear as if under it, releasing the ball the moment the cup is lifted. With the student's knowledge

Fig. 52

of palming, he can see how easy it is to use the above apparatus, and can, in place of one ball, use two or even three, and,

FIG. 53

if using his wand, can appear to take them from off the tip of his wand each time he feels so inclined.

The Ball Box

The box consists of three portions, as shown in fig. 54, and is usually made of boxwood. The case is accompanied by a small solid ball of the same material. Commence by showing this ball and apparently placing it in the lower portion, but in reality palming it. Place the cover on and, again opening the box, clip the middle portion, which will remain on

the lower—it will appear as if the ball were still in the box. Place the lid on again, and lift it, this time bringing up the middle portion also; the box will appear empty. This can be repeated as many times as the performer thinks fit, alternately showing the box empty one moment, and the next showing the ball apparently in it. The trick can be concluded by finding or producing the movable ball from any place the performer chooses.

FIG. 54

The Red and Black Ball Vases

These vases are usually worked in pairs, and are somewhat similar to the ball box, as shown in fig. 55. Each vase is provided with a different colored ball, one having a black ball, and the other a red ball. The center portion, or shell of a ball, is in one vase painted black, and in the other vase red; thus, if the red ball is placed in the former, it can be apparently changed into the black one, and in the latter, if the black ball is placed in it, it will apparently be changed into the red one. This change can be repeated as often as the performer thinks fit, eventually taking the balls out, and showing them as first placed in the vases. The vases can also be made to appear as if they contained each a red ball, or each a black ball, as the performer chooses.

FIG. 55

To Change a Ball into a Rose

The apparatus for this trick is in the form of a vase, as represented in fig. 56, and the vase is provided with two black balls, one solid and the other hollow and made in two halves. In the hollow ball is placed a rosebud, and the closed ball is then placed in the *pochette*, ready for use. Provide a similar rosebud, which show, with the solid black ball, to the audi-

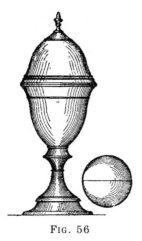

FIG. 56

ence. While they are examining these, secretly take the prepared ball from the *pochette* and, opening the box, show it empty. Receiving back the rosebud and the solid ball, pretend to pass it to the hand holding the hollow one, which immediately show. Place this one in the box and, taking the rosebud in your left hand, attach it secretly to a small hook, fastened to a piece of elastic passed up the sleeve, and drawn down and hooked into the bottom of the coat sleeve in readiness, and then inform your audience that you will cause the ball and the rose to change places. Place the cover on the box and, bringing the two hands together, still showing the rosebud and saying, "One, two, three! Pass!" let it go, and it will immediately fly up your coat sleeve. Then open your hands to exhibit the solid black ball. Now open the box, which acts with a spring, working from the top and bottom of the box, and in lifting the cover you lift off the upper half of the hollow ball, leaving the rosebud inside, which take out and show your audience, and they will really imagine that such a change has taken place.

The same apparatus, made on a larger scale, is useful in restoring borrowed articles.

The Obedient Walking Ball

This trick, of Oriental origin, uses a large wooden ball with a hole bored through it, not straight, but as shown in fig. 57.

Through this hole pass a fine rope or thick cord, and tie a knot in each end to prevent its coming off. Of course, the performer can, in show-ing the ball, have the cord out of it and, in sight of the audience, pass the cord through the hole in the ball. The ball will run easily back and forth on the rope.

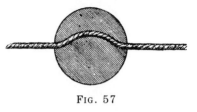

FIG. 57

Now, taking the ball at one end of the rope, place your foot on the other and hold it almost perpendicular, and allow the ball to slide down; you can cause it to stop instantly by simply drawing the rope perfectly tight, and upon again slackening it the ball will again slide down the rope. This can be repeated as often as the performer chooses, causing it to walk a few inches along the rope and then stop, and then to go on again, by tightening or slack-ening the rope.

CHAPTER 8

TRICKS WITH HATS

Suitable Introduction to Hat Tricks

I intend to devote the present chapter entirely to hat tricks and apparatus used in connection with them. The performer, before commencing, should have a small parcel placed in his breast pocket on the left side of his coat, containing a wig, a pack of cards, and a few other small things, which can be placed inside the wig, and which can be taken hold of secretly and quickly.

Stepping forward, the performer borrows a gentleman's hat; taking it in his left hand and holding it close to his left side, he turns to return to the stage, and in doing so apparently stumbles, which causes him momentarily to bend his body. Quickly taking hold of the parcel with the right hand and drawing it from his breast pocket, he drops it into the hat. The turn and stumble will attract the notice of the audience, who will not see him thus drop the parcel. Regaining his upright position, he moves on as if going toward the stage, but apparently casting his eyes downward, he professes to see something in the hat. Turning to the audience, he tells them the reason he stumbled was the heaviness of the hat, which seems to be loaded. This will cause quite a sensation, because being still amongst the audience, they

would never imagine that he had already placed the articles
there. He then takes out the articles one by one, making various remarks as he does so, bringing last of all the wig out
of the hat. This causes a great deal of amusement, and pre-
pares the audience to expect greater marvels.

I will now deal with the various articles that can be produced from the hat, when the performer returns to the stage
with it.

The Cannonballs

On the *servante* of your table, have placed two so-called
cannonballs, one of which should be solid and the other one
hollow, as in fig. 58. This hollow ball is so made that one
half slides partly around the other half, and should be filled
with a number of multiplying balls, so made that they can be
compressed flat, as shown in fig. 59. Have this ball closed
and placed alongside the solid ball on your *servante*. In
each ball a hole is made in which to place the tip of the finger, thus enabling the performer to bring the ball up inside
the hat. Having borrowed a tall hat, walk to the back of your
table and show it empty. Continuing your remarks, allow
your hand holding the hat to drop down gradually to
the back of the table, as
shown in fig. 60, and, holding the hat opening down
over the ball, slip your
finger into the hole in
the ball, and bring it up
into the hat. At the same

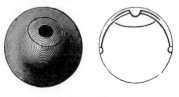

Fig. 58

FIG. 59

moment turn the hat opening upward and, walking from the table, profess to notice something heavy, and shake the ball out onto the floor; being solid, the ball will make a convincing sound as it falls. Placing the hat opening down again on the back of the table, step forward and pick up the wooden ball.

Now, taking up the hat as before, but this time introducing the hollow ball, bring it forward as if to return it, when you appear to notice something else in the hat and, placing your hand inside, slide the moving portion of the

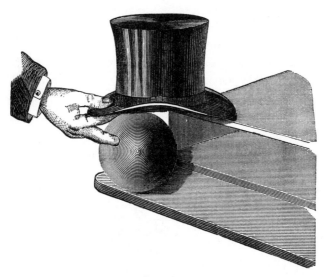

FIG. 60

hollow ball around, leaving an opening from which you take ball after ball, until the hollow ball is empty. Close it again, and produce the second cannonball, which *do not drop* on the floor, but place it on your table beside the other one, and the audience will imagine that as the first one was solid, the second one must be solid also. The hat can now be returned to its owner, brushing it before handing it back.

This illusion is a very grand one, as the large balls alone are each sufficient to nearly fill up the inside of the hat. The hollow ball can also be filled, according to the will of the performer, with such things as soft feathers, which, being compressed into the inside, will, when produced, appear a large quantity. You can also place inside it bonbons, small toys, or a number of small articles, instead of the compressed or "multiplying balls."

A Dozen Babies from a Hat

These are specially made, being compressible, and having a spiral wire up the center, as shown in fig. 61. They are all like dolls in appearance, and are made of colored muslin. These dolls can be produced from the hollow cannonball previously referred to, or can be introduced in any way the performer thinks fit. When you are preparing them ready for a trick, compress them all together one on the other as flat as

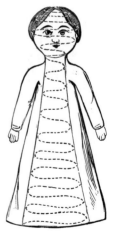

Fig. 61

possible, and tie a piece of thread around them to keep them from opening out until you are ready for them.

To Produce a Hundred Goblets from a Hat

FIG. 62

Get a tinsmith to make you the required number of goblets of thin polished tin, about four inches in depth, tapering gradually down, as shown in fig. 62. Being thus made, they fit together very closely and occupy very little space. Have these put into a small black bag and placed on your *servante*, to be introduced into the hat, after producing some other articles as before described. Some performers place them in one of the side pockets, to be secretly intro-

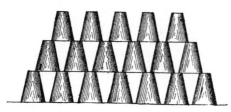

FIG. 63

duced in making a slight turn from the audience. In taking them out from the hat, do not place them one in the other, but as shown in fig. 63.

A Dozen Handbags from a Hat

These are specially constructed, so as to fold into a very small package. They are made of cardboard, covered with leather or some other material, and when opened they have

the appearance of an ordinary
handbag, as in fig. 64. Get a dozen
of these and fold them over flat, as
shown in fig. 65, and secure them
together by means of a piece of
black thread or an elastic band,
and have them placed ready for
introducing into the hat on your
servante or in your side pocket, as
described before. When bringing
them out of the hat, take the handbag by the ribbon and give it a
sharp shake so that it will fall into
shape, as shown in fig. 64.

FIG. 64

FIG. 65

To Produce Two Birdcages from a Hat

There are two or three descriptions of birdcages, but those
in general use are the kind I am about to describe, and
which are illustrated in fig. 66. The bottom is made to slide
upward, and the two sides next folding in upon the bottom,
and the ends upon these again, one over the other. When
closed, there is a space between the top (being slightly oval)
and the bottom, when the cage is folded up for use, to hold
a live canary. These are placed with the flat ends together,
and put on the *servante*, ready for introducing into the hat
in the usual manner.

When producing the cages from the hat, after they have
been introduced into it, take the hat in the left hand and
hold it down slightly behind the table; then, drawing one of

FIG. 66

FIG. 67

the cages quickly out, take hold of the ring at the top and give the cage a smart shake, when it will fall into position, as shown in fig. 66. Place this on the table and produce the other in the same manner. Some performers produce them from their vests, but the *servante* is the best mode to use in introducing them into the hat. The birdcage closed, ready for introducing into the hat, is shown in fig. 67.

To Produce Two Hundred Yards of Colored Ribbon from a Hat

For this trick, obtain about six yards each of six bright colored cloths, and, cutting each piece into six strips, join the ends together by sewing, so as to form two long strips of equal length. Roll each strip up very tightly and place one in each of the secret side pockets of your coat. Introduce them into the hat, as described before, in making a slight turn of the body away from the audience, and, making some remark to the owner of the hat in regard to its lining, tell him it seems a strange kind of material to have his hat lined with.

Taking the end of the strip, quickly pull it out, unwinding the roll as you do so, letting it fall onto the floor. When the first roll is finished, introduce the second in the same manner, and when it is all unwound, it will seem almost an impossibility to your audience that such a quantity should have been produced from the hat, as the stage will be covered with it if you take care to throw it well around you as you unwind it from the hat.

CHAPTER 9

MISCELLANEOUS TRICKS

Under this heading I intend to describe a number of tricks not described in the preceding chapters, and which are adapted some for a drawing room only, and some for the stage. I shall commence with the simplest tricks and illusions first.

The Miraculous Candles

This is really a very simple illusion, and only fit for a juvenile audience. Obtain a large apple, and carefully cut it in two pieces to represent the shape and size of a piece of candle. Cut two small slips from an almond, fix one into each piece of apple, and, having these ready, place them each in a candlestick. Now light the wick, or small piece of almond, and it will burn like a common candle. Say that, being rather hungry, you trust the company will excuse you if you venture to take your supper in their presence; at the same time picking up each supposed candle, blow them out and place them one after another in your mouth. Of course, knowing what they are composed of, you will eat and swallow them, to the apparent horror and disgust of your audience.

To Cut a Piece off a Person's Nose

For this illusion, get two knives, alike in form, but in one have a gap made as in fig. 68. Have the knife with the gap in it behind your table, and also a small piece of sponge dipped in port wine. Now request a lad to step forward and to be seated, as you intend to cut off his nose. Show the first knife, and allow it to be examined.

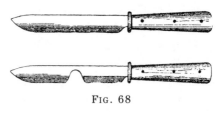

Fig. 68

When it is returned to you, walk up to your table to pick up a small cloth to tie around the lad's neck, and in doing so exchange the knives, picking up the one with the gap, but taking care that the audience do not see the difference, and in your left hand have the small piece of sponge concealed. Fasten the cloth around the boy's neck, and, taking his nose with your left hand, pretend with the right to cut the lad's nose, letting the gap slip down upon it, squeezing the sponge with the left hand at the same time. It will appear as if the blood were running down his face, and as if the knife had passed nearly through the lad's nose.

When you think it has caused enough fun, pull off the knife and place it with the sponge on the back of your table. Remove the cloth and wipe the lad's face. Nothing has happened to his nose, much to his surprise and that of the audience. If any person wishes to examine the knife, take up the one without the gap, and wiping it on the cloth hand it to be examined.

To Pass an Egg into a Bottle

For this experiment steep an egg in strong vinegar or acetic acid for about twenty-four hours, which will make the shell soft and pliable. Show your audience a real egg, and taking it to the table exchange it for the soft one, and showing a glass bottle inform your audience you will pass it through the neck inside the bottle. You will find it a very easy matter to do this, and when inside show it to your audience; and now saying you will take it out, hold the neck of the bottle downwards over a goblet half filled with water, and gently knocking the bottle the egg will fall through into the goblet, and upon going into the water will resume its former hardness.

This is a capital illusion if only carefully performed.

The Cut String Restored

FIG. 69

This is a neat illusion for the parlor or drawing room. Obtain a long piece of string and show it to your audience. Fold it, making it in the form of a double loop as in fig. 69, and keeping the finger and thumb of your left hand over the fold. Now request some person to cut the string between the loop, and when he has done so, tie the left end. While he is doing this, pretend yourself to tie the other end with your teeth, but at the same time pulling out the small piece of string which has been cut off, and concealing it in your mouth. Now hold the loop with your left hand and, taking your wand in your right, touch the string, commanding it to be whole. Upon opening the left hand and exhibiting the string, it will appear not to have been cut.

The Mysterious Columns

The apparatus for this old-fashioned trick is shown in fig. 70. Holding the two pieces together as in the figure to the left, take the string and pull it through back and forth. Now get some person with a sharp knife to cut between the two columns at the upper part, as if cutting the

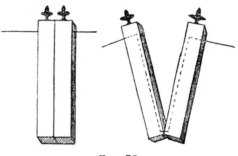

FIG. 70

string through, which, upon exhibiting, it will appear as if it has really been cut, though in reality it has not, as the string does not pass through the top, but down each column and out through the bottom. Now place the columns again together and, touching them with your wand, command the string to be again perfect. Upon again pulling the string, it can be again drawn back and forth, thus appearing as if the string were again united.

The Mysterious Balls and String

This illusion is a very old one, but is always well received. Obtain three wooden balls and bore through the center of

FIG. 71

each a round hole large enough to pass two cords through easily. Now get two pieces of stout cord about twelve feet long, and fold each one double, as in fig. 71, and thread the three balls on the double cords, allowing the center ball to cover the fold in the cords. Now request two persons to step forward, and, tying the cords as shown in fig. 72, hand each person two ends. Placing them opposite each other, tell them to pull sharply when you count "three."

Taking up your wand, say, "One, two, three," at the same moment each person pulls sharply against the other, and to their surprise the balls will drop to the floor, and the cords will be perfectly straight, the two ends each remaining in the hands of the holders.

FIG. 72

The Chinese Rope, Coat, and Rings

This illusion is an improvement upon the above, and has a much better effect. Obtain two pieces of fine rope, each about twelve or fourteen feet long, and tie them together in the center with a piece of black silk. Have two large brass rings, and commence by requesting three persons to come on the stage, and giving two ends of the rope to one person, and the two other ends to the other person, keeping both ropes held *well together*, request them to pull the rope to see that it is sound. When they have done so, take the rope from them, holding it by the center, and, walking toward your table to pick up the rings, fold each rope over as shown in fig. 73, and tie the rings exactly in the center, letting the portion of the ropes tied together with the silk be underneath the inner part of the rings, while the

FIG. 73

knot is outside. Ask the third person to take off his coat and pass two ends of the rope down one sleeve, and the other two ends down the other. Now request him to put his coat on, but this time having the back of the coat toward the front, lifting the rope with the rings tied in it over the person's head, so as to let the ring fall exactly between the shoulders. Draw the ends of the two ropes tightly, and place the person's hands behind him, and in this position tie an ordinary knot (single), the ends of the two ropes passing down each sleeve allowing of this being done. Show your audience that his hands are really tied behind him; and now, placing him with his face toward the audience, stand exactly at the back of him and, taking the ends of the rope, *reverse* their positions, so as to bring the ends passing down the right sleeve toward the *left-hand* side, and the ends passing down the left sleeve to the *right-hand* side, and hand these ends to each of the other two persons, requesting them to hold them tightly, and to pull sharply when you call "Three." Keeping your left hand placed on the person's left shoulder, take the rings in your right hand. Saying "One, two, three," give the rings a sharp pull, breaking the silk thread and releasing the rings. At the same moment, each person pulls the ends he is holding with a sharp movement; the ropes will pass down the sleeves and appear perfectly straight, and free from the knots tied in them, while you exhibit the rings also free from the rope in your right hand.

This is a capital illusion, but will require a deal of practice on the part of the student before he can accomplish it dexterously.

The Magical Mirror

This illusion is really a marvelous one. Provide yourself with an ordinary looking glass, about sixteen inches long by eight inches wide, and obtain a piece of hard chalk, sharpen it with a knife, and draw upon the surface of the glass any design or words you think fit.

After having written on the surface of the glass, take a silk pocket handkerchief and lightly wipe the face of the mirror. The surface of the glass will appear to be without a mark of any kind, and perfectly clear. Having this ready, bring the mirror forward and introduce it to your audience, showing it to them with a clean surface. Request some lady to gently breathe on the face of this looking glass, upon which the characters and designs you wrote upon the glass will be instantly visible. You can again wipe it off carefully with your handkerchief, and upon another person breathing upon its surface again, the writing will be again visible. This can be repeated as often as the performer chooses.

To Pull Yards and Yards of Paper from Your Mouth

Obtain several sheets of colored tissue paper and cut them into strips about an inch wide. Glue them end to end, and when dry, roll up the lengths thus obtained into several small coils, leaving a piece projecting from each center. Fill a large plate with cuttings and scraps of the same sort of paper, and have this on your table. Conceal the coils of paper in your hands and, being ready, request a boy or girl to come on the stage, and ask him to partake of supper with you. Hand him some of the paper cuttings to eat, taking some yourself and pretending to eat them, and take the opportunity of slipping into your mouth one of the small coils. Taking the end, draw it out of your mouth, telling the lad to do the same, which of course he cannot do.

When the first coil is finished, place apparently in your mouth a few more of the paper cuttings, at the same time under cover of your hand slipping in another coil, which you produce as before, and continue this until you have finished all the coils you have palmed.

Blood Writing on the Arm

For this illusion you must have a confederate sitting in the audience, and agree with him beforehand to write a certain

word on a piece of paper—for example the name "James."
Now draw back the sleeve of your coat and shirt, and with
a piece of soap, pointed fine, write the same word on your
arm, and draw down your shirt and coat sleeves again.
Have an envelope with a piece of paper in it and, bringing
this forward, request some person to write a word upon the
piece of paper and to seal it up. Your confederate, of
course sitting in front, takes the paper from you, and having written the word, which he takes care to show to the
others sitting near him, he places it in the envelope and
seals it up, and returns it to you. As soon as you have
received it, you hold it in the flame of a candle until it is
reduced to ashes. Now, turning back your sleeve, you rub
the ashes on your arm, and the ashes will adhere to the
soap marks, which your audience cannot see, and to their
astonishment the word "James" will appear as if printed on
your arm.

The Dancing Sailor

This is a figure of a sailor cut out of cardboard, the legs and
arms being attached to the body by means of a piece of
thread. Have a piece of thread drawn across the stage
(the thread will be invisible to your audience), and have this
thread passed over your table, at sufficient height to enable
you to fix on the sailor, allowing him to stand on the table.
At each side of the head is a small slanting cut (as in fig. 74),
and this is bent slightly back, forming a small hook, and
enabling you to fix it on the thread. At one side of the stage
your assistant has one end of the thread (the other end being
made fast to a nail), and he, being concealed from the audi-

ence, can agitate the
thread at pleasure,
causing the sailor to
dance, etc.

Bringing the sailor
forward, you intro-
duce it to your
audience and, mak-
ing some suitable
remark, you take it
to the table and
endeavor to make it
stand, but when you
let it go, it falls flat.
You do this a second
time, with the same

FIG. 74

result. The third time, you fix it on the thread, and it stands
upright. Taking your wand, you pass it slowly to and fro
over his head, and, turning, you ask for a little music, when
to the surprise of the audience it begins to dance, getting
quicker in its movements as the music plays quicker, and
stopping when it has ceased playing. You lift it off the
thread again, showing it to your audience, and explaining
that it has no connections whatever. Your assistant, meanwhile, giving the thread a sharp pull, breaks it off, thus
allowing you a free passage to the back of your table.

The Enchanted Dancing Skeleton

This illusion is practically the same as the last, the only difference being that the figure is cut out to represent a skele-

ton instead of a sailor. It can be made any size the performer chooses, and has been exhibited as a spiritualistic illusion by many performers.

Having the thread placed across as before, you introduce your skeleton with a few suitable remarks and, holding your

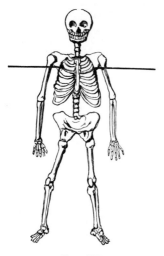

FIG. 75

wand, place the skeleton on the table, taking care to fix it on the thread by the arms, as in fig. 75. Ask for a little music, and the figure will move as the sailor did, but will look much more grotesque. Now borrow a gentleman's hat, and place it under the skeleton, which will dance inside, while you take your wand and apparently pass it right around the figure, but in reality only pass it around the front.

Take the hat away and lay the skeleton flat on the table. The moment your back is turned the figure rises slowly up, but when you turn around, it again falls. Seeing this, you again lay it flat, and place your wand across it as if to keep it down; but as soon as you turn again, the figure springs suddenly up, throwing your wand on the floor. You step to your table and take it by the head; your assistant at the moment breaks the thread, and you bring the skeleton forward to the audience.

This illusion, if properly worked, will create a great amount of fun and merriment amongst the audience.

To Produce Eggs from a Person's Mouth

For this trick, provide yourself with five empty eggshells, and have these placed under the waistband of your waistcoat. Place in the mouth of your assistant a small egg, and, having all ready, step forward with a plate and inform your audience that your assistant is suffering from an overloaded stomach, and that, with their permission, you will relieve him. Placing him in the center of the stage, you hand him the plate, and at the same moment secretly take from under your waistcoat one of the concealed eggs. Palming it with your right hand, you pat your assistant on the head, and he gradually opens his mouth, and the egg is seen; the performer immediately raises his right hand as if to receive it, and as he covers the assistant's mouth, he closes it, the egg again going back. Exhibiting the palmed egg, the performer places it in the plate. Patting his assistant on the head as before, the performer, again secretly taking another of the concealed eggs from his waistcoat, produces a second, and so on until he has disposed of the five, and then, repeating the same movements as before, he takes the sixth and last egg *really* from his assistant's mouth. This illusion, if performed well, never fails to surprise the audience, as they naturally conclude that the eggs all came from the assistant's mouth.

The Magic Coffers

These are round tin boxes, and are generally worked in pairs. They are usually about six inches in depth, and made in three portions, as shown in fig. 76. For example, if the

FIG. 76

performer is using these boxes for changing one box of rice into a box of flour, fill one box with rice and the movable portion with flour, and fill the other box with flour and the movable portion with rice. Place the lids on the movable portions which they fit, and which, to all appearances, consist only of the lids.

Now show each box filled as above and, placing on the covers, inform your audience that you will cause the contents of each box to change places. Upon opening the box of rice and lifting off the cover, you nip with your fingers the lip or bottom edge of the movable portion, and to all appearance the box contains flour; now open the other box, doing the same as with the first, and the flour will appear to have turned into rice. These changes can be repeated as often as the performer thinks fit. These boxes are very useful in "ringing the changes" in working other tricks.

The Orange and Rice Trick

FIG. 77

For this illusion, provide yourself with two tin cones about ten inches in height, and both made apparently in the same manner, but in reality one is made perfectly plain inside, while the other is fitted with a little flap about halfway up, which, upon touching a spring, is caused to fall inward, as shown in fig. 77. Have both these cones enameled black inside and out. In the upper part of this cone have a quantity of rice. Next, obtain a vase, the bottom of which is movable and works with a spring, thus allowing the rice placed in the vase to pass into the inner compartment, as shown in fig. 78. This vase is made ornamental, and to the audience there is nothing about its appearance suggesting concealed mechanism. In this vase have an orange placed, and on your table have another orange, and a small paper bag filled with rice.

All being ready, the performer borrows a gentleman's hat, which he places on one of his small tables, opening downward. He next brings forward the vase and the paper bag of rice, emptying this into the vase as he does so, and taking the rice up in his hands to show it is really in the vase. The orange, being covered with the rice, cannot be seen. Placing the cover on this, he secretly, with his fingers, forces up the spring in the bottom of the vase, thus allowing all the rice to escape into the lower compartment. Placing this on the small side table, the performer produces an orange and, drawing attention to it, places it on his table, just over the wrist trap, and over this he places the plain tin cover.

Now, taking the other cone, with the rice concealed in it, he places it on the top of the borrowed hat, at the same time releasing the secret flap inside and allowing the rice to fall onto the hat. The performer now informs his audience that he

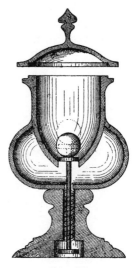

FIG. 78

will effect a magical transformation, and that the rice in the vase shall leave it and appear under the cover, on the hat. Taking his wand and touching the vases, he professes to take the rice out, carrying it to the cover over the hat, which he also touches with his wand.

Now lifting the cover from the orange, which is discovered as it was first placed, and placing both hands around it, he brings it over the wrist trap, pressing the trap at the same moment and allowing the orange to fall through onto the shelf beneath. He makes the motion of squeezing the orange smaller and smaller, and walking to the vase, making the pretense of passing it through the cover, and at the same time saying, "Pass," he opens his hands, which are seen to be empty. Lifting the vase now, the performer removes the cover and takes the orange out, which the audience will really believe has been passed into the vase. Walking to the other table, he lifts the cover from the hat, and the rice is seen, and the illusion is perfect, the audience really imagining the rice and orange have changed places.

The Flying Glass of Water

The apparatus required for this trick are a couple of ordinary glass tumblers, exactly alike, with a rubber cover fitting over one of them. Fill this one with water before putting on the cover, and when ready, place it in your *profonde* on your right side. Now get two large colored handkerchiefs of exactly the same pattern, and sew them together all around the edges, but in the center between the two handkerchiefs stitch a wire ring exactly the size of the tops of the tumblers.

Take up the empty tumbler and, in the sight of the audience, fill it with water, which you show to them, allowing them to examine it. Walking to the back of the table, put the glass down and, taking the handkerchief mentioned before, place the ring exactly over the top of the glass, and taking this in your right hand lift it up; at the same time, under the cover of the handkerchief, with your left hand place the glass of water secretly on your *servante*. As you then come forward, your audience will naturally conclude you are holding the glass of water, as

FIG. 79

shown in fig. 79. Suddenly taking the end of the handkerchief, you let go the ring, and throw or shake the handkerchief toward your audience, who will naturally expect a shower, but to their surprise the glass of water will appear to have vanished. Now select some person in the audience to come on the stage, and tell him you believe he has the glass of water concealed about him. Turning him round and round, and allowing him to stand for a moment between yourself and the audience, secure the glass from your *profonde* under cover of his body, and, removing the cover, lift up the back of his coat and apparently bring out from underneath it the glass of water, which you can show to your audience, who will take it for the same as that which you first showed them.

To Change a Bowl of Ink into a Bowl of Water

To perform this illusion, you will need a spoon with a hollow handle, as in fig. 80, having a little hole close to the top of the bowl portion of the spoon, and another hole at the top of the handle. This hollow you have filled with ink, which is retained within the hollow handle so long as the small hole at the top is covered over, but when uncovered it will run down into the spoon. Now get a large glass goblet and line the inside of this with black silk, damping it to cause it to adhere to the glass. Fill this with water and put a few gold-fish in it. Next, provide yourself with a large colored hand-kerchief and a white card, but this latter you must stain at one end of one of its sides with ink.

Having all ready, you introduce to your audience the supposed large bowl of ink, and to prove it is so, you dip the white side of the card into it, but in bringing it out you turn the card, showing the audience the side with the inkstain.

Now, taking the spoon mentioned above, you apparently dip it in the goblet, at the same moment allowing the ink to run down from the handle into the bowl of the spoon. Show this also to your audience, and they will after this naturally conclude that the water in the goblet is really ink. Place the handkerchief over the bowl or goblet, and tell your audi-ence you will now command the ink to change into water,

and lift up the handkerchief, at the same time nipping through it the black silk

Fig. 80

placed inside the goblet, and the water will be seen with the fish swimming about in it, and it will appear as if you had really changed the ink into water.

The Mysterious Pigeon

In your left breast pocket, place a small pigeon. Now commence by borrowing a tall hat and, while taking it to the table, turn suddenly around and ask for another one, and again walk to your table, but secretly drop the pigeon into one of the hats this time. Place this hat on the table and put the other one on top of it, placing them brim to brim. Now ask some person to lend you a coin, and inform your audience you intend to pass it into the bottom hat invisibly, and ask them how they would like it to fall, whether heads or tails up. Some will cry one and some the other; having the coin in your left hand, make the pass to take it in your right, but palming it, and taking your wand in your left hand, pretend to throw the coin toward the hat, at the same time opening your right hand to show it empty. Now request some person to step forward and lift the topmost hat, and ask him to say whether he finds it "heads" or "tails." When he lifts the hat, he will no doubt say it is both, and asking him to take it out, show the pigeon to your audience, much to their surprise. As regards the borrowed coin, the student will have no difficulty in producing this from some piece of apparatus already described. This trick requires the performer to show a great amount of humor and merriment in performing it.

To Produce Colored Ribbons from a Bottle of Water

The bottle in this trick is made of tin, with an enclosed space around the sides to contain wine or water. In the center is a tube with an opening in the neck, and at the top of this tube is a flat piece of metal perforated with small holes,

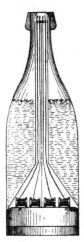

FIG. 81

through which the ribbons are drawn. This metal plate is fixed to a wire running down the center of the bottle, and fixed to a false bottom, which fits into the hollow or underpart of the bottle; on this bottom are placed, usually, four bobbins of colored ribbon, from which the ribbons are drawn through the holes in the plate mentioned above. The bottle is represented in section in fig. 81.

Have this ready on your table, and commence by showing the bottle and pouring out several glasses of wine, which you present to your audience. Now take the end of one of the ribbons and draw it out, and so on with the others, until the bobbins are empty, allowing the ribbons to fall on the stage in a heap, which will make the illusion look more surprising.

The Egyptian Pyramids

For this trick the student must procure first a small decanter, having in the center of the bottom a small hole, which is stopped by a pellet of wax. Next have two large wineglasses, and get three tin stands, one of which must be hollow and have a hole in the top. Now get three metal covers made in the shape of a pyramid or cone, as shown in fig. 82. One of these is made perfectly plain, but the other two are made with a compartment close to the top of the cone with an opening pointing downward; on the top of these two is an ornamental knob, which presses slightly inward, and is connected with a small rod running down the inside to the interior opening. Prepare these by filling one compartment with port wine and the other one with water. Fixing a small pellet of wax over the orifice or outlet, stand them on your table ready for use.

Commence by bringing forward a glass, into which you pour some port wine and some water, and when you have mixed it, pour it into the decanter. Now take a wineglass and place one on each of the plain stands, and place over each glass one of the prepared covers; as you do so, press the knob on the top of the cone, and it will force out the pellet of wax, and the wine will run into one glass and the water into the other. Now take the decanter, and with the finger under it, scrape away the pellet of wax placed over the hole.

Fig. 82

Place the decanter on the stand so that the hole in the decanter is just over the hole in the stand, and the wine and water will run from out the decanter into the interior of the stand.

Now, facing your audience, tell them that you will cause the wine and water placed in the decanter to separate and to appear in the two glasses, the wine in one glass and the water in the other. Upon lifting the covers off the glasses, the change will appear to have taken place, and the decanter will appear empty upon lifting the cover off it. This is a capital trick, and if worked dexterously it will cause a great deal of wonderment.

The Magic Funnel

This funnel is a large tin funnel made double throughout, the inner funnel being joined to the outer one at the top, and having a hollow handle opening into the hollow space between the two funnels. On the top of this handle is a small pinhole, which should be covered with a piece of gelatin, so

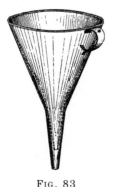

that it can be easily scraped off. The inner funnel is stopped at the bottom of the tube with solder, as shown in fig. 83. Prepare the funnel by filling the outer compartment with wine, which of course cannot run out while the air hole in the handle is stopped.

Now fill the inner funnel with water and, having all ready, bring it forward and show it to your audience filled with water, taking care to keep your finger

Fig. 83

over the bottom of the tube as if to prevent the water from running out. Pour the water out of the funnel into a glass, and show the funnel empty. Now request some person to step forward, and, handing him a tray with a few small wine-glasses on it, hold the funnel in the right hand and secretly scrape off the gelatin. Placing your thumb over the air hole, hold the funnel over one of the wineglasses. When you lift your thumb, the wine from the hollow space between the two funnels will run into the glass. When this glass is filled, place your thumb again over the air hole and the wine will cease running. This you can repeat until the wine has all run out. A great deal of fun can be created, by the performer who has just taken a glass of it a moment before. I might mention that the funnel should be enameled black inside and out.

To Change a Bottle of Wine into a Vase of Flowers

For this experiment you must procure a tin bottle, made in appearance to represent an ordinary black glass bottle, but hollow for about three-quarters of the inside, and having a bottom fixed just below the shoulder of the bottle, as shown by the dotted line in fig. 84. The upper part of this bottle will hold about three glasses of wine. Have the bottle enameled black.

Now have a small vase made of tin, and inside have fixed a spiral wire spring, so that it can be forced down inside the vase. Have the top of this spring soldered to a round plate of tin, which can rise to the top of the vase, but which is prevented from coming out by having a wire rim soldered inside the top. Get a small bunch of artificial flowers and

FIG. 84

glue or fix it onto the top of this movable plate, so that when pressed down it will go inside the vase. The bottom of the vase must be made flat, and just large enough to fit inside the bottom of the bottle. Paint or decorate the vase according to fancy; have a cardboard cover made to fit loosely over the bottle, as shown to the right in fig. 84.

Having placed the vase inside the bottle, and poured some wine into the top compartment, commence by introducing to your audience the bottle of wine, holding it at the bottom to prevent the vase from slipping out. To prove that it contains wine, pour out three glasses, which you hand to your audience. Now show the cardboard cover, allowing them to examine it, and place this over the bottle.

Take up your wand, and touching the cover, tell your audience you will command the bottle of wine to be changed into a vase of handsome flowers. Having repeated the usual formula, take the cover near the bottom and, nipping it tightly, lift it up, at the same time bringing the bottle with it, and the vase of flowers will be seen in its stead. When released, the flowers will stand much higher than either the bottle or the cover, thus making the trick appear all the more marvelous to your audience. Still holding the cover, let your hand fall for an instant behind your table, allowing the bottle to slip from the cover onto your *servante*, and having done so you can bring the cover forward again to be examined, as well as the vase of flowers.

To Change a Box of Bran into a Bottle of Wine

For this trick you must procure two boxes made of tin, of the form shown in fig. 85. These boxes are exactly alike in appearance, although one is in reality a box, but the other is open at the bottom, and up the inside to the shoulder or rim around the box, which is placed near the top, and at which is a partition within the box soldered to the inside surface. Paint both of these boxes black, and fill the first one full of bran and place it on the front of your table. In the

second one, place some bran in the top compartment, thus causing it to appear full of bran like the other.

Inside this bottomless box you have a specially constructed bottle, so made that the neck can be forced down the inside, as in fig. 86, and which has a hollow compartment in which you place a few glasses of wine. This bottle is

FIG. 85

Fig. 86

Fig. 87

painted black and, when released, rises from the inside by means of a spiral spring, and appears to the audience as if it were an ordinary glass bottle, as shown in fig. 87. Since it is black, they cannot notice any peculiarity about it. This bottle has a small catch or pin near the bottom, and the box, when placed over it, fits over this pin by means of the notch shown in the engraving to the right in fig. 85, and by giving it a slight turn, it is held fast. Now have a cardboard cover made to fit closely over the tin box.

Place the prepared box on the back of your table out of sight, and commence by showing your audience the real box of bran, turning it out to show that it is full. Allow them to examine it, and, receiving it back, walk to your table for the cover, at the same time exchanging the boxes. Hand the cover to be examined, and, placing the box upon your table, put the cover over it. Now tell your audience that you will command the bran in the box to disappear and a bottle of wine to appear in its place.

Taking the cover, nip it tightly, turning it slightly so as to release the box from the catch on the bottom portion of the bottle. Lift it quickly, bringing up the false box with it and leaving exposed the bottle of wine, which will resume its shape the instant the false box is lifted off. Being taller than the box or cover by two or three inches, it appears a most marvelous transformation to your audience, especially when they see you pour out the wine contained in the bottle. If anyone in your audience wishes to examine the cover, walk to the back of your table, and in taking it up, allow your hand to drop and release the false box, which will fall onto your *servante*.

The Drawer Box

This box is of frequent use to the performer, in producing or causing to disappear any article or articles; it can be made of any size the performer chooses. Boxes of this kind are also of great utility in enabling the performer to produce, apparently from an empty box, a large quantity of toys, etc., to be distributed amongst the juvenile portion of your audience.

In appearance this box is nothing more than an ordinary drawer, made of any kind of wood; it is, however, made double, having two drawers, one working within the other, as shown in fig. 88. At the back part, and just on the underneath portion of the outer box, is a small spring, which, if pressed in, prevents the inner

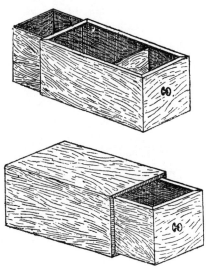

Fig. 88

drawer from being drawn out, while the outer drawer, being drawn out about three-quarters of the way, is shown empty. Upon again closing the drawer and releasing the spring, the drawer, if again pulled out, will bring with it the inner one, and it will then appear as if the drawer has been instantaneously filled with miscellaneous articles.

The whole of the interior of both these drawers should be painted black, while the outer box or casing can be painted or decorated according to the fancy of its owner.

The Unfolding Drawer Box

This style of box is not unlike the one described above, the inner drawers being made double and working one in the other, as in the last; but this box, instead of having a flat top, is made in a raised form, as shown in fig. 89. The top, to all appearances, is made in this shape for the sake of ornament, but in reality it is hollow and closed with a flat slab, the hollow space being filled with various articles, and the slab fixed in its place or released at will by means of a spring at one end of the top of the box. The box is

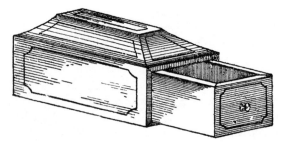

Fig. 89

unlike the other in this particular: it is made in such a manner that it can be opened and the inside exposed to view in the manner shown in fig. 90—the top and sides working on small hinges, and when pressed together again fitting together in the proper shape and form, by means of a number of little pins fitting into corresponding holes, thus holding the parts firmly together.

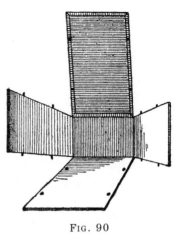

FIG. 90

The inner drawer having been filled and placed in the box, the performer commences by showing the box empty and, closing it, releases the spring at the bottom. Upon opening the drawer again, it is seen full of articles. The drawer is emptied and taken out, and the box is then pulled apparently to pieces, as above, to show that there is nothing else concealed. Fitting the box again together, and replacing the drawer, the performer commands the box to be again filled, at the same time pressing the spring on the top, which releases the slab; it falls flat into the bottom of the inner drawer, and the articles concealed in the lid fall upon it, covering it entirely. The drawers are now again pulled out, upon which the box will appear to be again mysteriously filled. The whole of the interior should be of one uniform color, black being the best, as it makes an illusion more perfect.

Changing Caddies

These are made in various modes. The simplest is an ordinary wood box, about six inches in length by four in height and width, having a transverse bar across the top. Within this box is a movable compartment, which will, by sloping the box one way or the other, slide from end to end. The inside of the box is closed by two small lids, one for each compartment. In the movable drawer, place an article, for example an egg, which should be either hard-boiled or blown.

Having this ready, the performer displays the box and, lifting one of the small lids, shows the compartment below

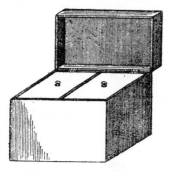

FIG. 91

perfectly empty; placing the lid on again and closing the box, he gently slopes it, causing the drawer to slide under the compartment just opened.

Opening the box again, he lifts the small lid as before, upon which the box is seen to be occupied by the egg. This arrangement can be understood by referring to figs. 91, 92, and 93. This class of caddy is only available for appearances and disappearances.

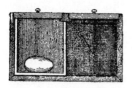

FIG. 92

For causing transformations, another caddy is brought into use, having three compartments, as shown in fig. 94, with a sliding drawer occupying two of these compartments. The caddy is shown in fig. 94 with the sliding drawer toward the left. Opening the small lids over these compartments, you place in the center one an orange, for example, and in the other a quantity of peas. Placing the small lids on again, you

FIG. 93

close the box, and by sloping it slightly you will cause the drawer to slide down toward the right side, thus bringing the peas into the center compartment and the orange into the right-end compartment, as in fig. 95. This can be repeated as often as the performer chooses; it is therefore obvious to the student that the caddy can be used to great advantage in changing any particular article.

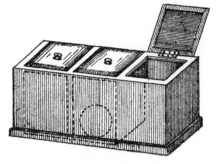

FIG. 94

There is another kind of caddy, known as the "skeleton caddy," in which the bottom is made

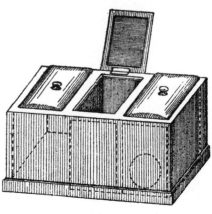

FIG. 95

to take out, thus allowing the audience to see through all three compartments; in this case the sliding drawer is bottomless, and is so made that it will only slide when the performer releases it by touching a spring fixed in the molding around the bottom of the caddy.

There is yet another kind of caddy in which the sliding drawer is moved forward and backward by means of a small pin projecting through the bottom, and working in a narrow slit cut in the bottom of the caddy. This kind is more often preferred, as the performer has no need to incline it one way or the other.

The Magical Caddy and Vase

This apparatus is used to cause a borrowed handkerchief to change places with peas. For this you require first a caddy, somewhat like an ordinary tea caddy, with three compartments, as shown in fig. 96. This is made with a hollow space or false bottom, as shown in the illustration, and is furnished with a sliding drawer, working on this bottom from end to end; but this drawer has only a bottom to one compartment, as shown in fig. 97, so that when this open compartment is over the opening in the center of the false bottom, it will allow a handkerchief to be placed apparently in this compartment, but in reality in the space between the two bottoms.

In the compartment of the drawer that has a hollow bottom, put a quantity of peas, and in the false bottom place a substitute handkerchief, and allow the compartment with the peas to slide under the center, ready for use. Next, provide a tin vase made in three portions, as in fig. 98. This

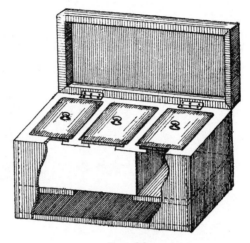

FIG. 96

vase should be about ten inches in height and have a foot or stand, as shown in the diagram; the center and movable portion is made to fit exactly over this, but having a well-shaped center fitting into the interior of the vase proper, and occupying about three-quarters of its depth. At the bottom of this center portion, and on the outside, is a projecting pin, and the cover, also made of tin and fitting over the movable portion, has a little slot cut in the bottom edge, fitting over this pin, so that by slightly turning the cover it will catch this pin, and enable the performer, in lifting the cover, to lift the center portion with it. Now fill the well-shaped space in this center portion with peas similar to

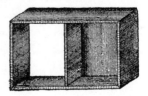

FIG. 97

those placed in the caddy, and place the cover over it, as before mentioned.

Having the necessary apparatus ready, the performer commences by borrowing a white handkerchief. Taking the vase, he shows it empty, placing his wand inside to show that it is so. Placing the borrowed handkerchief in this, he puts on the cover, inside of which is the center portion, filled with peas, and placing it on his table, he gives the cover a slight turn, releasing it from the pin on the other portion. The performer now shows the caddy, opening and showing each of the side compartments empty, and the center one filled with peas. Putting on the small lids over each compartment, he closes the caddy and places it on his table, at the same time sloping it and causing the sliding drawer to move, thus bringing the opening over the handkerchief. Addressing his audience, the performer says he will now command the handkerchief to change places with the peas, and after the usual formula he opens the caddy and brings out the substitute handkerchief, which he exhibits, placing it on his table; he now lifts the outer cover from the vase, upon which the audience, seeing the inner portion filled with peas, will conclude the change has really taken place.

Placing on the cover again (taking care to catch the middle portion this time), he walks to the caddy and, taking the handkerchief, says to his audience that he will now attempt a more difficult feat, to cause the handkerchief and peas to return to their former positions. Placing the handkerchief in the center and *open* compartment of the caddy, he secretly pushes it under the false bottom and pulling on the lid again, he closes the caddy, gently sloping it to cause the peas to come under the center. Opening again, after the usual magical formula, he lifts the cover from the vase, taking care to bring with it the center portion, and placing his wand inside his vase, he produces the handkerchief, and upon opening the caddy, the peas are seen in the center compartment as at first, the other two compartments being shown empty. Returning the handkerchief to its owner, he replaces his apparatus and the trick is completed. Great care should be taken by the student that in sloping the caddy and in catching the outer cover on the center portion of the tin vase, it should be done without attracting the attention of the audience.

The Inexhaustible Box

In outward appearance, this is an ordinary box made of walnut, mahogany, or any other kind of wood, and usually about sixteen inches in length and about twelve inches in width and depth. Internally, the width and depth, exclusive of the lid, must measure the same. The bottom is made movable, working upon a couple of hinges fixed on the front, and so arranged that if the box is stood upon its front or face, the bottom falls flat, as shown in fig. 99. Inside the box, fixed also to the front, is another piece of wood exactly the same size, and glued to the outer bottom at right angles, so that when the box is placed on its face, and the outer bottom falls flat, the inner bottom occupies the same space, and to the audience it will appear to be the real bottom. When the box is closed, this piece lies flat against the inside

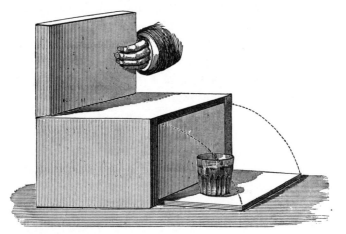

Fig. 99

of the front portion of the box. The inside of this box is painted black throughout.

The performer commences by showing that the box is empty, and placing it on the table as shown in fig. 99, in which position the audience sees inside the box, while the performer secretly places an article upon the real bottom as shown above, and closing the lid, he stands the box on its bottom, taking care not to lift it, but simply turning it over, and in doing so the false bottom is brought flat against the front side of the box, and the article placed on the outer bottom is thus brought inside the box, from which the performer takes it and exhibits to his audience. Again showing the box empty, he repeats the same as many times as he thinks fit, bringing out an endless number of things, apparently from an empty box, which the audience sees is empty after the production of each article. The articles to be introduced into the box should be placed upon the *servante*, from whence they are taken with the left hand under cover of the box, and placed upon the bottom as before described.

The Demon's Cauldron

This illusion is very effective, but is only suitable for the stage. The apparatus is very ingeniously constructed, usually made of copper or brass, polished outside and painted black inside. To all appearance it is an ordinary metal cauldron, but it is so made that it is constructed in hollow chambers inside, and having a bottom chamber with an outlet, which must be secured by a small screw plug. The cauldron will be better understood by referring to fig. 100. The bottom chamber is made to contain water, which, being

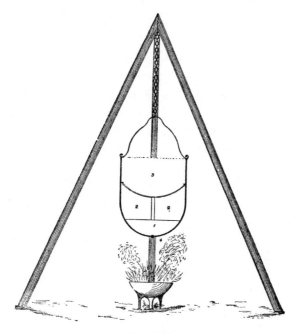

FIG. 100

poured into the cauldron at the top, passes through a small tube running through the center of the other chambers, usually three in number, and made to contain birds, rabbits, guinea pigs, and so forth. A circular plate revolves over these chambers, with a piece cut out to enable the performer to take out the animals, etc. This plate is shown in the uppermost illustration in fig. 101. The three chambers are all made the same size, but an opening is left at one side, where there is space for a fourth chamber; but this is covered, as in the lower illustration of fig. 101, by metal blackened over, so that when the circular plate is drawn around, the opening in it comes exactly over this closed chamber. Between these chambers and running through the center is a small round table into which a small metal plug is placed, so that it can be removed quickly, or replaced, as required. Three wooden poles, of sufficient length to act as a tripod, and connected at the top, should be made, from which a strong chain and hook can hang, to enable you to hang the cauldron on it.

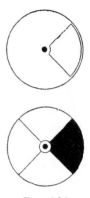

FIG. 101

Provide a metal cover to fit the top of cauldron, and inside the three hollow chambers place the birds and animals you intend to produce, and turn the circular plate around to conceal them. Commence by placing the tripod stand on the stage, and, bringing on the caldron, show it to your audience. Turning it toward your audience, show them the inside; but as this is blackened, the audience cannot perceive its shallowness.

Hang up the cauldron upon the hook and chain and, producing a bucket of water, show it to your audience. Take several eggs (say six), and break each one and turn the contents into the inside of the cauldron. Placing your hand with the wand inside the caldron, secretly remove the plug from the tube, and pretend to beat up the eggs. Now pour the bucket of water slowly into the cauldron, and when the bucket is empty, show it to your audience. Place the cover on the cauldron, and place underneath it a tin containing some cotton wool, spirits of wine, and red fire, and set fire to it.

Commanding the water to turn into air, and the eggs to

bring forth life, lift the cover and, placing your hand inside, turn the circular cover around, bringing the opening over the first chamber, and produce its contents; do the same with the second and third, until you have produced the whole. Turn the cover around as before to cover the three chambers, and fit the plug into its place. As you produce all the various animals and birds, pass them to your assistant to take away. Lift down the cauldron and, turning it toward your audience, show it empty. This is a very magnificent illusion, but it must be performed with great care.

To Cause a Rose to Appear in a Glass Vase

The apparatus for this trick is a glass vase on a foot, having a glass lid, and standing about ten inches high. This is fixed on a narrow wood box, ornamented according to fancy. The back of the vase has a piece cut out, and the back of the box is open, through which a curved wire arm works up and down, describing a half-circle. The end of this wire has a clip to receive the stalk of a real flower, and this, being placed in readiness, is set free by pressing a stud on the top of the box, releasing the spring and causing the wire to spring up, bringing the rose inside the vase, as in fig. 102.

The performer commences by introducing to the notice of his audience the glass vase, and, stepping forward, borrows a lady's handkerchief. Throwing it for a moment over the vase, he touches the spring; upon lifting the handkerchief the rose is seen inside the vase, and the performer, lifting the lid, takes out the flower, which he hands with the hand-kerchief to the lady from whom he borrowed it.

FIG. 102

The Chinese Ring Trick

These rings are usually made of polished brass, and made in sets of from six to twelve. Each set consists of one or two key rings (these being split to allow the other rings to be passed onto them), several single rings, a group of two, and a group of three. Many changes can be made with these, the audience naturally imagining that the rings are all *single* rings, as you hand only these to be examined.

A glance at the engravings will give the student an idea of some of the forms in which the rings can be linked together. The rings marked *1* are single rings, those marked *2* are the double linked rings, and those marked *3* are the treble

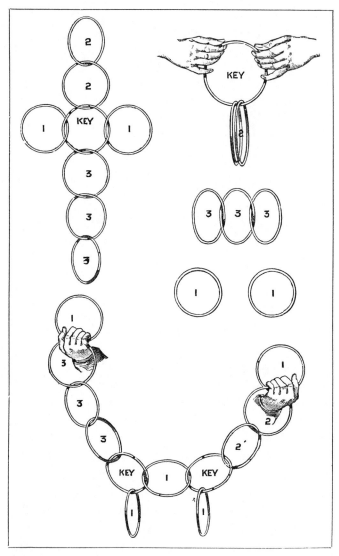

FIG. 103

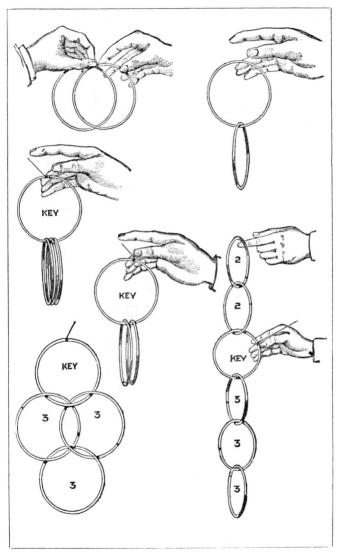

Fig. 103a

linked rings, while the key rings are marked "Key." The different positions in holding them are shown in fig. 103.

Great skill is required in performing with these rings to do it dexterously and to deceive your audience; and a great amount of practice is required, which, when attained, will repay the student, because this illusion, if neatly performed, is always well received by any audience.

CHAPTER 10

STAGE TRICKS AND ILLUSIONS

Apparatus for Stage Tricks

Stage tricks require costly apparatus, and in most cases are worked by mechanical means, which enable the conjurer to perform such tricks and illusions as would be impossible for him to do in giving an entertainment in a drawing room.

The principal apparatus in stage magic consists of mechanical tables, some of which are specially made for the working of some particular trick. There are three classes of tables, however, always in use for stage tricks, namely, trap tables, piston tables, and electrical tables, but it frequently happens that a single table is fitted with all three.

The Plain Trap

There are many kinds of traps in use, and of these I will describe first of all this "plain trap," which is made circular and fixed to a surface plate, and screwed onto the top of a table. It is usually made of zinc or brass, and by the action of a spring hinge is pressed up level with the surface of the table, and is worked by pressure from the top, so that when an article is pressed upon it, the trap instantly opens inward, allowing the article to fall inward upon the hidden shelf beneath the top of the table, the trap immediately closing again as soon as the pressure is removed.

This class of trap is sometimes worked by means of a fine cord attached to the center of the circular flap, the cord being pulled either by the performer himself or his assistant. Thus, for example, the performer places a certain article upon the trap and, having put a cover over it, walks from the table. The assistant instantly pulls the cord, causing the flap to fall, and allows the article to fall inward upon the shelf. Upon releasing the cord, the trap rises instantly to its place. The performer, coming again to the table, lifts the cover, and the article has vanished.

The Wrist Trap

The next form of trap is the wrist trap. This trap is also worked by pressure upon its upper surface, and is not unlike the other in design and make. Also made of metal, it is circular in shape, hinged to a surface plate, and has two hinges, one plain and the other a spring hinge. The working is slightly different from the other, as the pressure is not upon the trap itself, but upon a certain portion of the surface plate. (See fig. 104.) In causing the disappearance of any article, for example an orange, it is put upon the trap, and the hands placed round it, as though about to pick it up or squeeze it. When

FIG. 104

pressure is applied upon the spring, the orange instantly falls through, the trap closes again immediately, and, the hands being lifted in the act of holding the orange, the performer walks as if to place or pass it into another piece of apparatus. Upon opening his hands it is seen that they are empty.

Dove or Rabbit Trap

The next form of trap is that known as the Dove trap or rabbit trap. Oval in shape, it consists of two flaps divided down the center (see fig. 105). These flaps are made to fall inward by slightly pressing the animal or bird upon them, and they immediately close again when the animal has passed through. Below this trap should be placed a box, padded at the bottom with hay or wool, to prevent the animal or bird from being hurt by the sudden fall. This box also prevents it from reappearing, which it would do if the space under the tabletop were left entirely open, so as to permit it to roam about at will. It is usual to have a wire bolt on the inside, to secure these traps

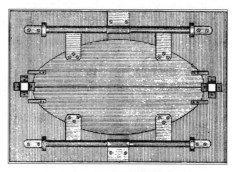

FIG. 105

until they are required for use, otherwise some article placed incautiously upon them would disappear when not required to do so. These bolts are usually made of stout wire, and worked from the back of the table.

The Changing Trap

The three traps above described are for the purpose of effecting a disappearance; but I shall now pass on to describe a more complicated kind of trap, known as the changing trap, which is not only used for causing a disappearance, but for replacing one article with another. The trap in this instance has an oblong surface plate about twelve inches long, with a circular opening in the center; below this plate are fixed vertically two round cylinders, so arranged as to work back and forth in a slide, so as to bring one cylinder under the opening, which a second before was occupied by the other cylinder (see fig. 106). These two cylinders are fixed to each other so that one cannot be moved without moving the other. They are worked from the back of the table by means of two rods, and each cylinder is fitted inside with a metal piston, moved up or down by means of these rods; and these pistons are so regulated by means of a spring as to rise gently upward and fit into the opening in the surface plate. Thus any article placed in the cylinder upon the top of the piston can, by the movement of the lever, be brought onto the surface of the

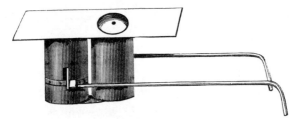

FIG. 106

table. I will now, for example, give the mode of changing an egg for an orange.

In the innermost cylinder an egg is placed in readiness; the performer, putting an orange upon the circular piston on the table, places over it a cover and gently lowers the rod, upon which the piston falls into the cylinder. He now pulls the other rod toward himself, bringing the egg under the opening; then, on raising the rod slightly, the piston from the farther cylinder is forced upward to the surface of the table, and upon lifting the cover the egg is seen in place of the orange, which was placed there a moment or two previously. Thus it is an easy matter for the performer to substitute one article for another, and he can also produce an article under an empty cover.

There is a small trap also made underneath in a cylindrical form, for causing the disappearance of six or eight coins, where it is necessary for the performer to obtain possession of marked coins, for a trick to be described later in this chapter, "The Crystal Cash Box," and for other tricks, in all of which the performer of course has an equal number of substitute coins palmed in readiness.

After the coins are collected, they are taken from the plate or tray, and placed in a pile upon the small trap; the performer, in the apparent act of picking up these coins from the table with the hand in which the substitute coins are palmed, presses a little pin, which allows the coins to fall slowly into the small cylinder below the opening, and another disc revolves and fills up the small round opening. The coins can then be taken out by the assistant and placed by him in the apparatus in which it is proposed to cause their reappearance.

The Bellows Table

This class of table has a double top, the upper one being a fixture, with a wooden trap opening upward, to allow a person to apparently disappear. The portion underneath is movable, and pressed close up to the top, when not in use, by the action of springs fixed in the legs of the table; this lower portion is, however, made like a bellows, and will sink down according to the weight of the person who gets upon it. The bellows part is made of cloth, nailed around the front and sides of the table, but open at the back. Such tables are usually provided with a long cover reaching nearly to the floor, so that before being used, the cover being lifted up, the audience can see right through and underneath the table, the movable portion being forced close to the top by the action of the springs mentioned above.

Smaller round tables are made upon the same principle, and are used mostly for the disappearance of small animals. The style of table can be understood by looking at figs. 107 and 108. The cover hangs three-quarters around the top, but is open at the back, as in the larger one, and the bellows portion, in its normal

Fig. 107

state, is pressed close to the top. Upon the top of the table is fixed a trap, to allow an animal to be pressed through, and when it falls through, the weight of the animal causes the bellows to expand. This type of table is usually provided with a wrist trap.

Having now explained the tables, and the traps and pistons fitted to them, I shall now proceed to explain a few stage tricks.

Fig. 108

The Magic Picture and Chosen Cards

This frame is held in the hand and has a glass fixed into the front, which, if a slight pressure is put upon its surface, causes an inner blind to release itself from the catch and spring suddenly upward. The back of the frame has a picture of some kind fixed to it, and has three tiny pinpoints projecting from it by which three cards can be fixed onto it. The roller blind, having a similar picture pasted onto it, is drawn and fixed to a spring at the bottom. In front of this, as mentioned above, is a piece of glass, thus causing the whole to appear like an ordinary picture, framed and glazed. When the spring blind is released, it springs upward and is quite concealed. This frame is brought onto the stage and shown to the audience, and the performer, taking a pack of cards, requests some person to draw three cards, taking care to force the cards required. The chosen cards are returned to the pack, and are then shuffled. Some person is requested to hold the frame, and the performer, standing in front, throws the pack of cards smartly against the glass of the picture frame, upon which the spring is instantly released and the three chosen cards are seen inside the glass. The performer now takes the frame and, removing the back, picks off the three cards and hands the frame for examination, taking out the glass also, and the audience of course fails to find the secret of the trick, as the roller blind is made to work in the thickness of the frame, and is therefore out of sight when the frame is examined.

The Magic Bell

This apparatus is used by performers for answering questions yes or no, and also for indicating chosen and drawn cards. This bell is made of glass, as in fig. 109, and is usually hung between two uprights fixed to the back of the table, and fastened to the back table legs, up which legs the connecting wires are taken, and terminated at top with two metal hooks. The cords of the bell (which in reality are cop-

FIG. 109

per wires covered with silk) are fastened or hooked onto these little hooks, and the assistant has only to connect the circuit by pressing the stud mentioned above, which will cause the hammer to rise slightly and strike the glass bell. Some performers have the bell suspended in midair, in which case the connections are made to wires passing through the ceiling, worked in the same manner.

The Crystal Cash Box

Two kinds of these boxes are in use, but I shall describe the one to which preference is usually given, and which is made all of glass, top, bottom, and sides, fixed to a light metal framework, having an ornamental design upon the top made also of metal. The box is about ten inches in length and five inches in breadth and depth. The top is made to slide out, giving access to the inside. Upon this lid, and immediately under the ornament on the top, the borrowed coins are placed, as shown in fig. 110; it will hold eight pennies or quarters; slips of glass are cemented to it as shown, to assist in keeping the coins in place. The front of the box is made double, the inner part being attached to hinges in the frame. This movable side is folded up under the top or lid, and keeps the coins in place until released by means of electric current. This flap is held in position by a small piece of black cotton passed through a tiny hole and around a platinum wire, which, when the current is applied, is heated red hot, and the cotton is instantly burned, and the flap falls, as shown in fig. 111, and releases the coins. This box is prepared by the assistant off-stage. The top having been slid off, the flap is folded up and secured to the opposite side by the piece of cotton, as described above, and the box is turned over to slide

Fig. 110

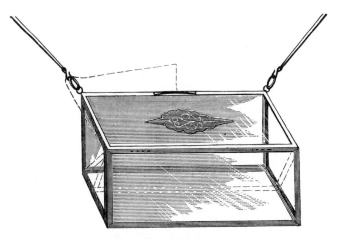

FIG. 111

the lid, with the coins placed in position, back to its place, and the box is then turned into its proper position and brought onto the stage and hung between the uprights of the table.

The mode of operation is as follows: The performer, having borrowed eight pennies or quarters, substitutes an equal number of his own for theirs, and the assistant immediately secures the borrowed coins and places them in the box as described above. The box is brought forward and, after being shown, is suspended from the cords, and is swung to and fro. The performer, placing the substitute coins upon the small coin trap already described, apparently picks them up, but in doing so presses the spring and the coins sink into the table. Closing his hand as if still holding them, the performer raises it as in the act of throwing, and, making a corresponding motion each time, says, "One, two, three! Pass!" and the assistant, pressing the stud, causes the electric current to release the flap, which falls, and the coins are seen and heard to fall inside the casket, from which they are taken and returned, thus appearing to have been thrown invisibly into the interior.

The Demon Drum

This is an ordinary drum in appearance, but fitted inside with two hammers, one at each end, which are set in motion by an electric current. This drum is usually suspended from the ceiling over the stage, and in sight of the audience, but it can be suspended between upright rods fixed to the table. In this case, two connecting wires are required to cause the double action within the drum, which can be made to give a single rap or a continual roll by the pressure of one or both studs. With a little practice, these drums can be made to keep time with a tune played upon the piano or by a brass band. The drum is also used for answering questions yes or no, for the assistant, being at the back of the stage can hear all the questions put, and answer accordingly. In the case of naming the pips upon a chosen card, it is necessary that such cards should be forced, the assistant knowing beforehand what number of raps to give.

The Electrical Table

This table is made to allow the glass bell or crystal casket, etc., to be hung from between the rods fixed to the table, as shown in fig. 112. These tables are to be procured at any

FIG. 112

first-class conjuring shop, but the student could, without very much trouble or expense, fit the necessary apparatus to his ordinary conjuring table.

The Aerial Suspension

This trick has been now before the public for many years, but when performed it always causes a considerable sensation. The apparatus required is, first, a kind of iron corset, for which the performer doing this trick must be properly measured and accurately fitted, according to his or her size and build. This corset is strapped upon the body, and attached to it is a rod passing down the right side from beneath the arm, almost to the right knee. Below the arm is a projecting piece so made as to fit into a socket, and almost in the shape of a crutch; and the rod passing down the side of the performer is so constructed that when a person has this apparatus strapped securely upon him or her, and the projecting piece under the arm is fitted into the socket of the pole, the body can be raised, and the toes in rising will describe an arc of about 90 degrees, assuming the position shown in fig. 113. To effect this, two poles are required of the same length, one made of wood and the other of iron, the latter being fitted into a socket in the stand, and having also a socket in the top, in which is fixed the projecting piece under the arm, and this rod therefore supports the whole weight of the body during the performance. The two poles are both painted the same color, and to the audience both appear to be the same.

The performer will have to provide a specially made costume to suit the working of the apparatus. The young lady (we will imagine that it is a lady who performs this suspension feat) is brought forward by the performer, and the two rods are shown, and a stool is placed on the stand on which the lady steps. The iron rod is now placed in position and fixed under the right arm, and the wooden rod is placed under the left; the performer, now making a few passes with his hands, apparently sends the lady into a mesmeric sleep, and gently draws the rod from under the left arm and lays it

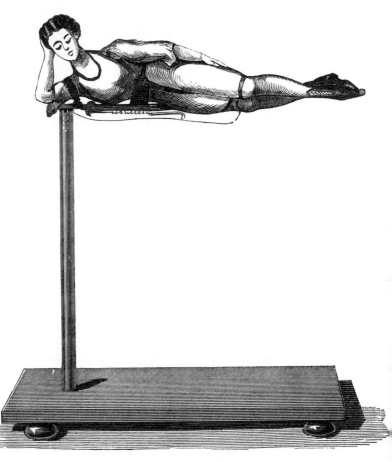

Fig. 113

down. Making a few more passes, he gradually raises the body of the lady into a horizontal position, and she will appear to be suspended almost in the air. With a little practice the body can be placed into any position.

When the lady has been suspended long enough, make a few more passes, and gently lower the body until in an upright position, and again place the wooden rod under the left arm and place the stool beneath her feet, and, taking a handkerchief, wipe the lady's face, and she will appear to awaken, and will step down from her exalted position.

An improvement has lately been introduced into the apparatus whereby the iron column is hollow, and through the center another rod is worked from beneath the stage, and in the socket of the iron rod at the top are placed a number of teeth which catch corresponding teeth in the projecting piece under the arm. This, being worked from below the stage, will cause the body of the lady to rise slowly into a horizontal position without being so placed by the performer. This is certainly a very great improvement in the mode of working, as while the performer simply makes a few passes with his hands, the body gradually rises, apparently without any visible means whatever.

The Indian Basket Trick

This trick also is a very old one, but of late years it has been improved upon by many performers. I shall describe two methods of carrying out this feat.

The first is performed upon a table or bench, constructed after the manner of the table used for the "Sphinx" or "Decapitation" trick, to be described next. The basket is made with a movable bottom, which opens inward and will fold up against the front. It is usually about five feet long by two feet in depth and breadth. The top of the table it is placed on is fitted with a trap, to allow the person to leave the basket, and pass through the trap, closing it. Then, under cover of the mirror front of the table, the late occupant of the basket passes down through another trap in the stage, and reappears a few moments after in some other portion of the building. When this kind of basket is used, it is lifted off the table, after the disappearance of the inmate, and shown to the audience.

For the second mode of operation, a basket of about the same size as the last described is used, but in this case it has two bottoms and is made precisely upon the same principle as "The Inexhaustible Box," described in the preceding chapter. The basket when opened is tilted forward, and while the other bottom lies flat on the stool or bench, the inner bottom is visible to the audience. It is usual to place the basket upon a low bench, as in fig. 114, in which the inner and outer bottoms of the basket are clearly shown.

The performer, in commencing this trick, usually comes forward with a young lady, dressed somewhat like a court page, and after having shown the basket, he places her inside and closes the lid. Taking a sword, the performer thrusts it through and through the basket, but takes care to do so in such a manner that the blade has an *upward* tendency. Screams are heard to issue from the interior of the basket, and blood is apparently seen on the sword blade, which is caused by means of a sponge dipped in port wine. The performer then opens the basket, and it is clear to the audience that it is empty. The occupant, however, is really

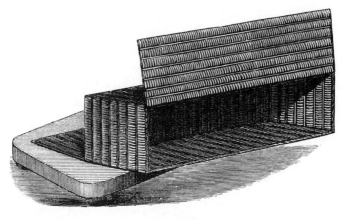

Fig. 114

lying flat on the outer bottom, concealed from view by the inner bottom, and when the basket is again closed, and turned upon its bottom, the young lady is once more in the interior of the basket.

Some performers, in doing this trick, have two young ladies, both dressed exactly alike, so that when the basket is shown empty, this second young lady appears in some portion of the building, and is taken by the audience for the one that entered the basket a moment or two previously.

The Sphinx or Decapitated Head

This illusion has been exhibited under various names, amongst others, that of "The Decapitated Head," and under that name it is most generally known to the public. The head of a man is shown on a salver upon a table, and is seen to move its eyes and open its mouth, and is even heard to speak, and to answer questions put to it. "The Sphinx" is a more pleasant form in which to exhibit this illusion, as it does not appear so ghastly to an audience.

For this startling illusion, the table is the most special piece of apparatus that requires description. To all appearances it is an ordinary table, but in reality it has only three legs, and on the insides of these legs are fixed two plates of mirrored glass, so fixed that when it is looked at from the front it appears as if one could look right beneath the table; the table is fixed in position as shown in fig. 115. The front leg (number 1 in the illustration) is placed exactly facing the audience, while the two back legs (number 2) are as shown. From the front leg to each of the two back legs a plate of glass is fixed in grooves made for that purpose (the glass is indicated as *G*). The top of the table is covered with some dark figured cloth, and in the center is fixed a small trap opening inward; through this trap the head of the person concealed below the table is placed. The table is placed in a curtained alcove as shown *(C B C)*, and the curtains at *C* are reflected upon each plate of glass, so that it appears to the audience to be the back curtains that they see. The per-

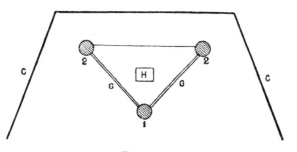

FIG. 115

son who is concealed below the table has a wooden collar fixed around his neck, and covered with cloth of the same pattern as the top of the table, and this collar, when the head is forced through the table, exactly fits the space occupied by the trap. The trap can be made either round or oblong, according to fancy.

The rest of the apparatus is very simple, being merely a bottomless box with the front made to fall down, which, when closed, is secured by a lock at the top. The performer, in advancing to place the box upon the table, must take care to advance in a straight line with the center leg of the table; if he stands either to one side or the other of the table, the glass will show the legs of performer reflected therein, and thus spoil the illusion. The lights having been lowered, the performer commences by introducing the box to his audience, saying that it contains the ashes of some person long since dead, but which at certain intervals can be called to life for a brief period. Placing the box upon the table, the performer steps forward and asks for a little low music. Returning to the table, he unlocks the flap of the box, which falls down flat upon the surface of the table, and the head is seen within, having been placed inside during the time in which the performer has stepped forward to ask for music. The eyes are seen to open slowly, and then the mouth, the head turning slightly to one side and the other. Questions are then put to it by the performer, and after the performance has continued long enough, the performer waves his hand and the eyes slowly close, and the box is again locked. Upon lifting it from the table, the latter appears in its normal condition, the person below the table having withdrawn his head and closed the trap the moment the box is locked. Of course, a great deal depends upon the talent of the performer and his assistant in regard to the questions and answers, as this portion makes the illusion more sensational.

The Globe of Fish and the Living Head

This is quite a new method of working the preceding illusion, and no doubt will appear more marvelous; but it has the drawback that the head is not heard to speak, but simply answers by motions, and the trick cannot be continued for so long. For this illusion you need to have specially made a large round fish globe, as shown in fig. 116, with a hollow made in the inside, opening from the bottom. This is made in the shape of a dome large enough to allow the head of a man to be introduced inside when the globe is placed upon the table. The dome should be about three-quarters of the entire height of the inside of the globe, so that the outer portion can be filled with water and fish, so that it appears to the audience to be really a globe full of water and live fish. The globe should be made about fifteen inches in height, and about fifteen inches in diameter across the widest part.

The bottom of the globe should measure about twelve inches in diameter, and the opening, to allow the head to be placed inside the hollow dome, should be about ten inches at the largest. This open-

Fig. 116

ing should be fitted with a round plate of glass, with the edges beveled to keep it in its position. With this the plate fixed in the bottom, the globe can be held upon the hands, thus making the illusion more perfect.

When the globe is being placed upon the table and over the trap, the assistant below opens the trap and the plate of glass fitting in the bottom falls into his hands. He can then place his head up inside the dome, and to the audience it will appear as if his head were really in the globe of water, the fish swimming around it making it appear still more marvelous.

Having all in readiness, the performer commences by bringing on the globe in his hands, requesting some person to see that it contains real water and fish. Placing it on the table, he borrows a large colored handkerchief or a small shawl and, throwing it over the globe, comes to the front and asks for a little soft music. He takes his wand and waves it slightly to and fro. Then he lifts the cover, and the globe is seen to be tenanted by the head of a man.

Questions can be put, which it will answer by nods and shakes of the head. After a few minutes the eyes close and the performer throws the shawl over the globe, and after again waving his wand to and fro, he lifts the cover once more, and the head has vanished. The globe can then be removed and brought to the front. Care should be taken not to lift it up, but to slide it forward to the front of the table, where one hand can be placed beneath it, in order to keep the movable plate of glass in the bottom from slipping and to hold it tightly in position. The plate that fits into the hollow space at the bottom of the globe should be made of very thick plate glass, about five-eighths or three-quarters of an inch in thickness. Great care must be taken, in performing this illusion, to always hold the globe in such a manner as to keep this false bottom in, because if it once slips, the illusion will be completely spoiled, the audience of course guessing the rest of the trick, and the manner in which it was worked.

The Living Head in a Bottle

The working of this illusion is in theory the same as the last, but in this case the head is contained in a large bottle or jar. This bottle should be made in the shape of a pickle bottle, and should be from fifteen to eighteen inches in height, and about twelve inches in diameter. It must be furnished with a false bottom, like the fishbowl just described, that can be placed in position and held by the hand being placed below it. This piece, being movable, is removed by the assistant when the bottle is placed upon the table, which allows his head to be passed up the inside; and by lifting the stopper from the neck of the bottle, questions can be asked and answered.

Having the bottle in readiness, the performer must now procure a head modeled in wax, made to resemble his assistant as nearly as possible, with the eyes closed, and with hair, whiskers, or mustache to match. This head is placed inside the bottle through the bottom. After replacing the loose bottom when the head has been introduced, the performer brings the bottle forward and shows it to the audience, explaining that the head within it is that of a malefactor executed a few years since, and that, by virtue of a secret bequeathed to him, the performer has the power of being able to animate it for a short period.

Placing the bottle upon the table over the trap, and borrowing a dark shawl, the performer throws the shawl over the bottle and, stepping forward, asks for a little soft music.

Taking his wand, he waves it to and fro, and, muttering a few magical words, lifts the cover. By this time the assistant, having opened the trap, has received into his hands the loose bottom and the wax head, and has replaced the latter with his own. The head that is now visible is to all appearance the same that has been already seen. Opening the eyes slowly, it yawns and makes other movements as if just endowed with life. The performer, lifting the stopper from the bottleneck, now asks questions, which the head answers. When this has continued long enough, the stopper is replaced, and as the performer waves his hands and wand to and fro, the eyes slowly close.

After placing the shawl over the bottle once more, the performer steps forward, making some suitable remarks to his audience, and then, advancing to the table, removes the cover and carefully takes the bottle off, sliding it to the front to enable him to place his hand under the loose bottom. The illusion, like the preceding two, requires the lights to be lowered about half. The illustration given in fig. 117 shows the shape of the bottle, with the wax head inside, and also the shape of the loose bottom.

Fig. 117

The Mysterious Head

This illusion has caused considerable sensation under various titles. The back of the stage or room is hung with a dark curtain, and hanging in front of this is a smaller curtain, which, when drawn aside, reveals a boxlike cavity about four feet from the floor, in which is seen the head of a lady. This head is apparently suspended upon nothing, being exactly in the center of the box, the back, top, sides, and bottom of the box being to all appearances visible; the head is endowed with life, and speaks and answers questions.

This illusion is caused, like the three previously described, by the aid of a mirror. An oblong boxlike frame

FIG. 118

is made, which is open at the front and bottom, and a sheet of mirror is fixed from the front edge and slopes back at an angle of 45 degrees to the top, as shown in fig. 118. In the center of this glass, an oval-shaped hole is cut, to allow the head of the young lady to be passed through; and around the edges of this opening, upon the surface of the glass, a piece of dark fringe about three or four inches wide is glued, the young lady herself wearing a piece of the same kind of fringe around her neck; this fringe prevents any shadow from being thrown upon the glass when the lady has her head through the hole. The top and sides of the box are papered or painted in diamond-shape designs, and the top is edged around the corners with a narrow gilt molding. When a light is placed in front, the reflection of the top and sides is shown in the glass, and thus it appears to be the bottom and full sides that the spectators see; and this causes the apparent illusion of seeing top, bottom, and sides, when in reality it is only the top and a portion of the sides that they can see.

The box is placed upon a stand behind the curtains, an opening being left to allow the audience to see into it, and another curtain is drawn across until the illusion is being shown, when it is drawn aside; the lights are placed in the front, at the lower edge of the box, which can be made from two to four feet across the front, according to fancy. Behind the curtain and below the box, a stand is placed for the young lady to either stand or sit upon when she is performing. Fig. 118 shows a side view of the interior of the box, with the head passed through the aperture in the glass.

The Bodiless Lady

This illusion is also a very sensational one, being in appearance the bust or upper portion of a lady resting upright upon a small stand placed upon a table, the spectators apparently seeing underneath the table, and also under the stand upon which the upper part of the lady rests. After having read the explanation of the illusion caused by the "Sphinx" table, the student will no doubt guess that this illusion is caused in a similar manner.

The table used for this purpose is made upon the same

principle, but has a piece cut out from the back part, to enable a lady to stand upright, apparently through the center of the table; the stand placed upon the top of the table is also made upon the same principle, being a small stool with three legs, and having the mirror placed from the front leg to each of the back ones; the top of the stand is padded, and covered to represent a cushion of some dark material, and has a space cut from the back similar to the table, to allow it to be placed around the front of the lady, thus causing the bust of the lady to appear as if it were resting upon the cushion of the stand. The top of the table should be covered with cloth of a dark color; the floor also should be carpeted with a carpet of *one* uniform dark color; and curtains, also of a dark color, say maroon or green, should be hung at the back and facing the sides of the table, as in the case of the "Sphinx." This illusion cannot fail to cause considerable sensation if properly worked, and many imitations of a similar nature have sprung up, all worked and planned upon the same principle; indeed, I could call attention to many if I had the space so to do, but the above description will suffice to explain to the reader that it is possible to cause the illusion of having the upper half of a lady apparently offered to view, either resting upon such a thing as a bar, or suspended so as to rest upon nothing or to be floating in space.

A Lady Suspended in the Air Without Any Visible Support

I have previously described what is known as "The Aerial Suspension," which has been considered a most remarkable illusion; but to see a young lady suspended in the air, about twelve feet above the stage floor, and without any support either beneath or above her that is visible, appears to an audience as far more wonderful and remarkable.

This idea was conceived by me some time ago, but circumstances prevented me from carrying it into effect. Not so with two other performers, however, who, having their hall entirely at their own command, were able to produce this wonderful illusion, which they did successfully, astonishing all who went to see it. I do not intend, however, to describe the method adopted by these two enterprising professors, but will explain my own mode of performing it, which is similar in almost every respect except one.

The curtain having been drawn up, the lights are turned partly down, the stage at the back being hung with dark curtains. The performer now leads forward upon the stage a young lady dressed in the fancy costume of a page, similar in appearance to the costume worn in "The Aerial Suspension," and, having introduced her to the audience, he leads her toward an ordinary couch placed in the center of the stage, upon which she reclines. The performer now professes to send her off into a mesmeric sleep. She slowly closes her eyes and appears to fall into a trance. He now straightens her limbs and places her hands across her breast, and then slowly removes the couch from beneath her, when she remains suspended, still in the same position. Now, taking a long wand, he slowly waves it to and fro in the air, at which the form of the young lady is seen to rise slowly upward, and does so until she is about twelve feet from the stage floor. Another movement of the wand, and the ascent of the lady is stopped. The performer now passes his wand to and fro beneath the lady to show that there are no supports of any kind.

With another movement of the wand, the lady begins to descend slowly until within about three feet of the floor, when the couch is again placed beneath her, and she once more resumes her former position upon it. The performer, putting down his wand, makes a few passes above her with his hands, and then slowly removes the hands from the lady's breast and places them by her sides; she now slowly opens her eyes and awakens as if from a trance, and rising she is led forward by the performer, bows to the audience, and retires.

During the whole of this performance, slow, deep, and solemn music should be played.

The mechanism required for this illusion is very simple in its construction, but must be very strong.

The couch is merely one of the ordinary kind, and without any mechanism.

Above it, close to the ceiling above the stage, and hidden by hanging drapery, are fixed securely three small blocks, two placed above the head and one above the foot of the couch. Through these blocks run very fine but strong steel wires, painted black.

Through the single block above the foot of the couch two wires are passed, and securely fastened at the bottom to a black leather loop, padded on the inside. Through the other two blocks is strong single wire, and at the bottom end of each wire is a very strong steel spring hook, also painted black. At each side of the stage, fixed to the wall, is a small but strong winch to which the other ends of the wires are taken, and by means of a small handle the wires are slowly wound up, causing the lady to ascend. These winches are fitted with catches to prevent them from unwinding. At each of them is stationed a man, who, at a given signal, commences to wind up the wire.

As regards the dress of the young lady, outwardly there is nothing unusual about it; but beneath the loose tunic she wears a thickly padded bodice, made stiff at the back by means of a stout piece of leather which is sewn onto the padded bodice. Across this bodice, and just below the armpits, a very strong leather strap is fixed and tightly buckled across her chest. Near the shoulders, and fixed securely to the strap at each side, is a stout steel ring; these rings are painted black, and when the outer jacket or tunic is put on, there are two holes made in front through which these rings pass, and the trimming is so arranged as to conceal them.

Having all in readiness, the performer introduces the young lady, and when she places herself upon the couch, the performer, in the attitude of placing her limbs straight, passes the leather loop over her two feet, and at the shoulders he secures the spring hooks to the rings projecting through the lady's dress, and then places her arms across her breast. The young lady has to stiffen her body and limbs as much as possible. The moment the couch is removed and the performer makes the signal, the men at the sides commence to wind up the wire slowly until the young lady has been pulled up to a sufficient height.

When the signal is given for the young lady to descend, the men at the sides take the catches off the winches and slowly begin to let out the wire, and the young lady slowly descends until she reaches the couch, which is placed in readiness to receive her.

These wires are entirely invisible to the audience, and if the blocks are well oiled, and the winding apparatus at each side is oiled as well, not the slightest noise will be made either in ascending or descending. The performer, in the act of putting the young lady's limbs into proper position again, unhooks the spring hooks from the two rings, and also takes the leather loops off her ankles.

This is rather a trying experiment for a young lady, and should not be prolonged too much; it is perfectly safe, however, if the performer takes care to get the proper wire. It is advisable always to test the wires thoroughly each day before the performance commences, as the performer should bear in mind that the young lady's life depends upon the wires; if one of them broke, it might cause another to snap also, owing to the sudden strain upon the remaining wires.

The "Thauma" Illusion

The body of the lady performing is supported on, and rests in, a kind of hammock, attached to the back of a cabinet, and is then affixed to a false wooden bust made to fit the bust of the lady, and thickly padded where the upper part of her body rests upon it. This bust is tightly strapped to the lady, across the shoulders and across the back. The bust is covered with silk or satin, and trimmed to represent a lady's low-necked dress bodice, with short shoulder sleeves. The remaining portion of the lady is encased in a dark-colored skirt (black velvet is the best), and her feet are firmly strapped to a wooden rest at the back of cabinet, as shown in fig. 119. The bust is supported upon a swing at the front

FIG. 119

Side view, showing false bust and hammock from false bust to back of cabinet, where it is affixed to a strong wooden rest, upon which the feet of the subject are supported.

of the cabinet. Four brass chains support a slab of wood about twenty-eight inches long by about eight to ten inches in width.

Midway up the chains at each side is a crosspiece of wood fixed to the chains, by which, when the lady grasps them with her hands, she can easily lift the bust from the wooden slab, allowing a sword to be passed beneath the bottom of the bust and the top of the wooden slab. When the lady is supported upon the swing she cannot swing *forward*, but can only swing with a slight *sideways* motion, because if she attempted to swing forward, the slab of wood would then no longer support the bust, and the performer would be in danger of breaking her back, as she would have no other support to sustain her, except the back of the cabinet, to which her feet are strapped.

The slab of wood forming the swing is made, in some cases, with two half-round holes, to allow the lady to place her hands through, to show that she can pass her hands beneath her.

The interior of the cabinet should be of one uniform color, if possible dark blue or dark maroon; it should be about six feet in depth by about five to seven feet across the front, according to fancy. The front should have either *dark* blue, maroon, or green baize curtains, so made as to draw right across.

On each side of the cabinet are affixed two lamps, as in fig. 120, with large plated reflectors, about ten or twelve inches in diameter. These should be so fixed that the curtains can be drawn at the back of them; and thus, when lighted, reflect a strong and powerful light *outward*, throwing the interior of the cabinet into deep and gloomy shadow. It must be evident, therefore, to the reader that the four lamps and reflectors play a very important part in making this illusion perfect, because, in consequence of a strong, bright, and dazzling light being reflected into the eyes of the spectators, it is impossible for them to distinguish anything inside the cabinet, beyond the bust and head of the lady.

The position for the lady performing is one of pain. In the

first place, she has to be tightly strapped to the bust, which causes difficulty in breathing and talking; and, again, the head must be held well back, to make it appear from the front as if the false bust and neck were completely one and upright.

Fig. 120

Front view, showing the positions of four lamps and powerful reflectors.

Many ladies performing this illusion cannot help showing in their look the pain and suffering they are experiencing even when before their audiences, thereby spoiling the effect the illusion would have had if their features had been composed and the face covered with smiles.

CHAPTER 11

CHAPTER 11

SPIRITUALISTIC ILLUSIONS, SÉANCES,
AND MANIFESTATIONS

Spiritualism: An Imposture

The days are past now for believers in spiritualism and spirit
manifestations, as the present age is growing more enlightened, and the majority of people look upon these feats as
being clever tricks, and the performer is applauded accordingly. It is the height of foolishness for any performer now to
stand before the public and profess to do such-and-such a
feat assisted by spirits, because the public would look upon
him as an impostor. It is not unusual, however, to find some
person more simpleminded than others, who really believes
what the performer says; but such people are indeed simple
and foolish to put their faith in such twaddle. I have included
this chapter not for the sake of exposing these feats, but simply as a guide for those who wish to amuse others, and who
in the first place must know how these feats are done before
they themselves are able to perform them.

The Sack Feat

This feat has astonished many, and will continue to astonish many more, because to see a person placed in a sack,
and the neck of it drawn together, tied, knotted, and sealed

by some person in the audience, and placed either in a cabinet or under a large cover which is thrown over the sack and its contents, and then to see the person step forth in the space of a few seconds entirely free and holding the sack in his hands with the knots still tied and sealed, is really marvelous to all beholders. For this feat, two sacks are provided, made of calico, both of the same size and alike in appearance. These sacks are made large enough for a person to stand upright within them and to be drawn and tied over his head.

The performer usually has an assistant to perform this feat; this assistant has the second sack concealed inside his vest. The performer steps forward and, after introducing his assistant and showing the sack, hands it to be examined, and requests some person from the audience to come on the stage. The assistant gets inside the sack, which is drawn up over his head. The performer, holding the neck of the sack with his hands, turns and requests the person on the stage to hand him the cord for tying the neck of the sack from the table; the assistant within the sack immediately withdraws the second sack from under his vest and forces its neck upward through the neck of the other, the performer apparently holding it tightly in the proper position for tying. Taking out his handkerchief, the performer passes this apparently tightly round the neck of the sack, but in reality he covers the edges of the *outer* sack, which is thus kept in its place and prevented from slipping. The handkerchief is tied and knotted, and the person with the cord is now requested to tie the sack with the cord, in any manner he thinks fit, the performer taking care that he does so *above* and not *below* the handkerchief. When the person has tied and knotted the cord to his own satisfaction, he seals each knot with wax.

All being ready, the assistant is laid down and covered with a large wrapper, and when this is over him he has simply to expand his arms and shoulders, which forces the outer sack from under the knotted handkerchief, and he is then free. Drawing the remainder of the sack from his vest, he removes the cover, taking care that the sack he has just emerged from shall be concealed in its folds, and stepping forth, holding in his hands the sack just drawn from his vest, with the knots and seals intact and unbroken, to the surprise of the audience. In removing the cover from the stage, care must be taken to lift up the sack concealed, and carry off the other in its folds.

The Spiritualistic or Animated Skull

The working of this skull, although apparently marvelous, is in itself very simple. The skull is made of papier mâché, and has a metal plate fixed from the base of the skull to the bottom of the lower jaw; with this exception, the skull is an exact model of a human skull, and is colored to resemble one. Through the back of the curtain a fine black silk thread is passed, the assistant behind the curtain having one end, while at the other end is a small piece of wood, around which is placed a pellet of soft wax. Two chairs are placed within two feet of each other, back to back, and across the backs of these two chairs is placed a sheet of glass, and upon this glass is placed the pellet of wax attached to the thread.

The mode of operation is as follows: The performer steps

forward with the skull, handing it for examination, to show that there is no concealed mechanism in it. Receiving it back, he places it upon the sheet of glass, *at the same moment taking the pellet of wax and pressing it hard against the base of the skull*, to which it adheres tightly. Now, taking up his wand, the performer commands the spirit to return for a brief period within the skull, and begins then to put questions to it, the skull answering "yes" by nodding forward, and "no" by shaking slightly to and fro. This is caused by the assistant gently working the thread, giving it a slight pull, which causes the skull to nod for "yes," and gently pulling the thread to and fro for "no," causing the skull to move slightly from right to left. Any number of questions can be asked; the assistant, being placed so as to hear them, can give what answer he thinks fit. If properly worked, a deal of fun and merriment can be caused amongst the audience by the questions and answers put to it. The skull can be picked up at any moment and brought forward to show that it is not connected to anything, the performer of course taking care secretly to remove the pellet of wax and drop it onto the glass.

The Spiritualistic Collar and Handcuffs

This particular feat requires the use of a light cabinet to place around the performer when he is executing it. The collar is somewhat like a large metal dog collar, and is made either of brass or of nickel silver, and is solid throughout. It works upon a hinge, allowing it to open in order to place it upon the performer's neck, this hinge being always kept in front. At the back of the collar are two metal eyes or staples through which a cord or chain is passed, and secured to a staple in the wall, or to a chair back. The collar has a secret way of opening, and the metal pin passing through the hinged part, although to all appearance in one piece and riveted through, in reality runs only three-quarters of the way through, and kept in its place by means of a spring, which is released by a small metal pin being pressed down a minute hole beside the pin, as shown in fig. 121. This enables the pin or bolt passing apparently through the hinge to be withdrawn, whereupon the collar falls in two, and, being fitted in its position with the bolt pressed home, the collar is free from the performer's neck without the fastenings behind being interfered with.

The handcuffs are the same as those used by the police, and two keys are provided, one of which the performer has in his possession, tied to the small metal pin for releasing the collar, and placed in his vest pocket, from which he can easily take them, although secured and handcuffed. The mode of operation, as worked by myself, was as follows: I stepped forward with the collar and handcuffs, a strong steel chain, and a padlock, which I handed around for examination, requesting some person to step forward from the audience to secure me. Taking the handcuffs, this person secured them on my wrists, keeping possession of the key after doing so. The steel chain, in the ends of which were two strong rings, was

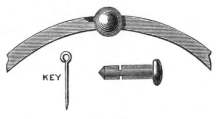

KEY

Fig. 121

passed around the back of the chair, and the collar was placed around my neck and secured with the padlock. The

rings in the end of the chain were placed over the two staples on the back of the collar, as shown in fig. 122. The padlock being locked, I secured the two staples, thus keeping the collar tight around my neck.

The curtained cabinet was then placed around me, and the curtain drawn in front. When I was thus con-

Fig. 122

cealed from the audience, I took the second key from my vest pocket, and, unlocking one shackle of the handcuffs, I drew off my coat and placed it across my knees, again securing the shackle around my wrist and returning the key to my vest pocket. The curtain was then drawn from the front, and I was discovered without my coat, still being secured as at first.

The fastenings having been examined, the curtain was then drawn in front, and I again took out the key and unlocked the shackles from both my wrists. Placing the small pin into the hole in the collar, I withdrew the bolt and took off the collar. Fitting it together again, I replaced the bolt, and then locked the handcuffs onto the collar. Replacing the key in my vest, I put on my coat and, taking the chair in my hand, stepped forth from the cabinet entirely free, the fastenings still being intact and untouched. The person who had secured me examined the fastenings again, and, being satisfied, handed me the keys and retired.

From the time of being first secured and placed in the cabinet to the time I stepped forth with the chair in my hand, occupied only about one minute. In this feat, any person in the audience can bring a padlock, and, no matter how complicated, it can be used in place of your own, making not the slightest difference, but causing the feat to appear more mysterious and marvelous to the audience when they see you step forth free.

Some persons, in performing this feat, are secured to an upright post from the back of the neck, and have their hands also handcuffed behind them and secured to the eye of a strong metal bolt by means of a cord or small chain. This bolt, to all appearance of one piece, can be taken hold of by the performer when his hands are secured behind him; by turning it slightly, the eye of the bolt can be withdrawn. In this case it is necessary to have a small pocket made at the back of the trousers to hold the second key, from which it is taken and the shackles unlocked by the performer, occupying but very little more time than the other way of performing the feat described above.

The Protean Cabinet

This cabinet is another adaptation of the principle of the "Sphinx" illusion, but in this case the mirrors are fitted to the inside of the cabinet. This cabinet is of wood, and eight feet in height by about five feet square, and supported on four short legs. It is made with folding doors, and inside is an upright pillar extending from top to bottom of the interior, and at the top of this pillar a lamp is fixed so as to show the whole of the interior to the audience. A movable mirror is fixed to each of the back corners of the cabinet and made to fold against this column, as shown in fig. 123, and when so fixed the mirrors reflect the sides of the cabinet, thus causing it to appear to the audience as if they can see the

whole of the interior. These flaps will also fold against the sides of the cabinet, and the backs are papered with paper of the same pattern as the whole of the interior of the cabinet, which is illustrated in fig. 124.

When the cabinet is first shown, the flaps are folded against the pillar, thus leaving a

Fig. 123

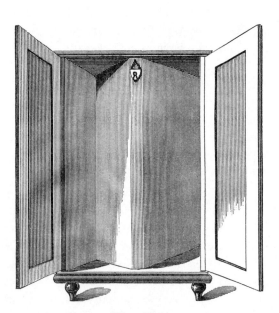

Fig. 124

triangular space behind the post, capable of concealing two or more persons. The performer comes forward with his assistant, who is placed in the cabinet, standing with his back to the pillar mentioned above. The doors are then locked, and two persons from the audience are requested to stand either behind or beside the cabinet. The doors are again opened, and a different person is seen, who steps forth from the cabinet, bows, and retires. The cabinet, to all appearances empty, is again closed and locked, and upon being again opened, another person, differently attired, is seen, who also steps forth and retires. The cabinet, again apparently empty, is closed and locked, and when it is opened a lady is seen standing within; she also steps forth, bows, and retires. The cabinet is again closed, and when it is reopened, the assistant who first entered it is seen, and he also steps forth, and the two gentlemen are requested to examine the cabinet inside and out. The assistant, before he comes out of the cabinet and while the doors are still shut, closes back the two glass flaps against the sides of the cabinet, where they are secured by a spring, thus allowing the gentlemen from the audience to examine the interior. Of course, being unaware of these movable flaps that are closed back, they fail to discover the secret.

The Davenport Brothers' Feat

For performing this séance, it is necessary for the performer to be able to release himself from the cords placed upon him to cause the various "manifestations." Feats of rope-tying are now very old, but the mode of working the remainder of the trick is more modern. Looking closely at

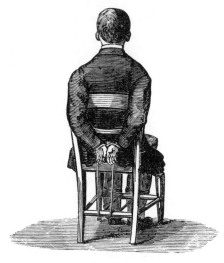

FIG. 125

fig. 125, the reader will notice the position in which the performer is tied. Obtain two pieces of rope about six yards long and, taking one in each hand, tie a plain knot, leaving about two inches from the top; tie another knot upon the top of that one with the long end, passing the end of the right knot through the left knot, and the left end through the right knot, thus forming a pair of handcuffs; let them be rather loose. Procure a wooden chair and, taking the rope, seat yourself. Take the ends which contain the knots, and let the ropes be placed under you at the back of the chair, passing the other ends under the lower back rail of the chair to the front to your knees, securing them. When the hands are strained, pass your hands and arms over the back of the chair; take up the ropes, twisting each one twice, and slip the hands through the loops, keeping them close together, so that the knot will be between your wrists. The rope from your wrists to your knees will be rather slack, but by bending the knees outward it will strain the rope tightly, so much so that it will leave its marks upon your wrists, and the more you bend the knees forward, the tighter and firmer the knots appear. When you are in this position and being examined, you must keep the ropes well strained. You must have an assistant on the stage to superintend the tying and knotting, and to point out where the knots are to be sealed.

To release yourself, loosen your legs, which will cause the rope to slacken, and you can then loosen the loops round your wrists, and withdraw your hands, placing the knot upon the seat; you can then take off your coat and vest and perform the various manifestations, and slipping your hands through the various loops, strain the rope again with your legs, and you will once more appear to be firmly secured. The Brothers Davenport did not use chairs but wooden benches, which were fixed into their cabinet, and had two holes bored through the seat, through which the ends of the rope were passed and tied to their legs. The knot at the back was made in the shape of two loops, as in fig. 126, through which their two hands were passed, and which were either drawn tight or slackened by the legs at pleasure.

Having explained the method by which the performer can release himself when tied up and secured, I will proceed with the further working of this trick. Provide a wooden cabinet about five feet in height, standing upon four short legs, and about five feet in length by four feet in depth. Inside, have a number of small hooks upon which hang

FIG. 126

various musical instruments, a drum, a tambourine, a guitar, a bell, and anything the performer fancies. In the door of the cabinet toward the top have a hole cut, through which can be seen and heard the various manifestations. The performer takes care to have all the instruments smeared with some luminous liquid, so that the instruments can be seen by him when shut up in the cabinet. When he has been tied up, and the doors of the cabinet are closed, the lights are turned down, and the performer immediately releases his hands, takes off his coat and vest, and, slipping his hands again into the loops, calls for "light," upon which the doors of the cabinet are opened and he is seen without his coat or vest. The doors being again closed, he releases his hands again and commences making a noise, first with one and then with another of the various instruments. Replacing his hands in the loops, he calls again for "light," and when the doors are opened he is still seen bound securely. The performer can continue the various "noises" and "manifestations" as long as he thinks fit, and can also have two persons from the audience seated in the cabinet, one at each side of him, for as it is all dark within, they cannot distinguish his various movements.

Different performers introduce various changes into their performances, but the foregoing will give the reader a correct idea of how this kind of séance is done, and he could therefore introduce many novelties himself in working the above when he has once mastered the way in which to release himself. The light of course must be turned right down immediately after the door of the cabinet is closed, and turned up again at the signal from the performer.

The Ghost Illusion

This illusion, which created a sensation in London, and was first known here as "Pepper's Ghost," I will endeavor to explain, and make the working of it as clear as I possibly can to the reader. It is caused by the figure of a man or woman being reflected upon a sheet of glass, and the audience, looking through this glass, apparently sees the figure upon the stage, but in reality it is not so, being only upon the glass.

In the first place a sheet of plate glass, perfectly clear and without a blemish, must be procured, and of such a size that it will show the image or reflection of the performer who impersonates the ghost. This glass is fixed at the front of the stage and inclined slightly toward the audience.

In front of and below the stage, a chamber is made, completely concealed from the eyes of the audience, but having an opening at the upper part, through which the reflection of the person below is thrown upward upon the sheet of glass. The reader can understand the position by referring to fig. 127.

The body of the person to be reflected is against an inclined plane, which is covered with black cloth. This inclined plane is fixed upon casters, and the person leaning against it, moving this slightly with his feet, either to the right or left, causes it to appear as if the ghost were walking either forward or backward.

Below the stage is placed a powerful lantern, the light from which is thrown upon the figure representing the ghost, thus causing it to be reflected strongly and brightly

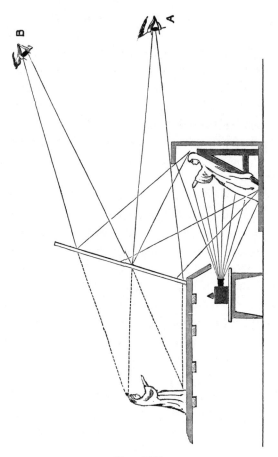

FIG. 127

against the glass fixed above. The stage must be darkened and dimly lit, otherwise the ghost will hardly be visible.

In making various motions of the body, the ghost actor must reverse his movements; for example, if he raises his left arm, the figure reflected above will appear to raise its right arm. The glass, as stated above, must be without a blemish, and fixed at an angle of 20 degrees, inclining forward toward the audience, and the nearer the spectators are seated to it, the larger the glass must be. The size of the glass depends upon the height of the figure to be reflected and the size of the stage and the theater or hall in which it is exhibited. This again will be understood by referring to fig. 127, in which A represents the eyes of that part of the audience seated in the lower portion or body of the hall, while B represents the eyes of those who are seated in the boxes or gallery, thus showing the angle by which the height of the glass is determined, as the angles of incidence are always equal to the angles of reflection, and the same angles of incidence are likewise equal to the corresponding angles of the reflected figure.

This illusion was invented in 1863 by Professor Pepper, by whom it was patented, hence the name "Pepper's Ghost," and for a long period it was exhibited at the Polytechnic in London, in various forms and guises, and drew thousands from all parts to see this wonderful exhibition. Although it cannot now be classed as a novelty, yet it still creates a great sensation whenever and wherever it is exhibited.

CHAPTER 12

THOUGHT READING

The Art Possible to All

It is really curious and astonishing to observe the readiness some persons display in ridiculing anything and everything they fail to understand. Thought reading is one of these, and people who fail to understand it simply put it down as trickery. Place before them the notion of some enterprise the accomplishment of which militates against the evidence of their former experiences, and they at once treat it with every form of derision conceivable, and at the same time feel highly indignant that such an endeavor should have been made to impose upon their credulity.

Take the experience of Mr. Irving Bishop as a case in point. He introduces to the notice of the public a unique and curious natural phenomenon, and a mental faculty and power which almost every person possesses more or less, but which is lying dormant and only requires cultivation, though at first sight it may appear to partake of the supernatural, or, as some of its opponents prefer to say, of omniscience.

What was the result of Mr. Bishop's experiments? He was received by a large section of the people with jeers, insults, and various expressions of disgust, terms being leveled at him of an unjust and un-English description. Mr. Bishop happened to be a conjurer, and therefore the popular notion chose to attribute to him an inherent inability to accomplish any really genuine feat without the aid of deception creeping in somewhere.

If he had come forward at first incognito, without his reputation as a conjurer being known, the probability is that his reception would have been different, and the spirit of opposition and suspicion he aroused would have taken a less demonstrative form.

Of course, since his first experiments in this country, we have others who have put the knowledge of this mental power more strongly before us, and have explained away a great amount of the opposition which was first shown to it, and amongst the names of those who have favorably done so is that of Mr. Stuart Cumberland, whose experiments with many of the leading men of the day are still fresh in the minds of most persons.

Planchette

Long ago, a little scientific invention known as the *planchette* was introduced, which was so constructed that the unconscious and involuntary action of the mental powers, when one touched this apparatus, caused certain results. The instrument consisted of a plain board, to which were attached two delicately constructed casters, and a pencil of sufficient length to mark a paper placed beneath it. The fingers of the operator were laid gently on the board, and by concentrating his whole attention on the experiment, the imperceptible action of his will upon the muscles of the hand caused the delicate mechanism of the board to produce marks on the paper which were accepted as answers to various questions asked.

There are people so foolish and superstitious as to believe that replies thus obtained were messages from another world, and many invariably applied to the planchette for advice before speculating upon any great event.

Thought Reading Explained

Thought reading is but the production, in a novel form, of a mental power recognized long ago, but very little attended to, until the experiments of Mr. Bishop caused deep-thinking persons to study and inquire into this apparently novel art. There is a curious drawing-room pastime, known as "willing," in which the combined will of a number of persons will compel one of the party to do what they desire and will.

Several persons gather in a circle and join hands, in one unbroken chain. A person previously selected and blindfolded is placed in the center of the group, and he is requested to make his mind a perfect blank—that is, to "think of nothing." It has been determined by the others, joined hand in hand, that the medium shall be "willed" to do a certain task, and whilst he is in the circle, each intently resolves that this movement shall be executed by him, the medium doing his utmost to dispel the various ideas, which, despite his endeavours, attempt to crowd before his imagination. If the experiment is strictly conducted under the conditions given here, the medium will suddenly break through the circle and execute the task desired, without being able to give any explanation of why he did so, except that he knew he had to do it, and of course had done so.

This experiment touches very closely upon thought reading, as is shown by the medium recognizing instinctively what he was desired to do, and the combined wills of those who stood around him being stronger than his single will, he felt compelled to do the thing desired.

How to Begin in Thought Reading

In thought reading, the success of all experiments is regulated by the susceptibility of those persons engaged, and by the adaptability they possess of firmly retaining mental impressions, a power which is quickly developed by continual practice. In the first place, the performer must be able to make his mind a perfect blank, and, a subject having come forward, he is requested, for example, to think of a group of numbers, and to think of nothing else. The performer takes this person by the hand, with his fingers resting upon the pulse, and asks the person to fix his mind intently upon the first number of the group of figures selected, and to think of nothing else whatever. The performer's mind being a blank, he simply fixes it to speak upon the subject, and the pulse of the subject will beat quickly the number thought of, then pause and go on again, beating the number upon which the mind is fixed, making a slight pause each time the required number of beats is given. The performer, feeling these beats, at once can detect the slight pause between each number of beats, and counts them, and naming it aloud, it will be found to be the number; go on again with the second, third, and fourth numbers, and the results will be the same. In commencing practice to attain the art, the performer should always begin with reading numbers first, and as the power becomes more fully developed within him, he can then proceed to read names and sentences thought of by his subjects.

Subsequent Progress in the Art

When the power is more fully developed, if a fine wire is placed around the wrist of the performer, and attached also to the subject, the result will be the same, as it acts like mental telegraphy, and the numbers or words become plain to the performer. The finding of a pin or any other article hidden by a person can also be easily carried out, if the performer puts himself in communication with the person who hid the article. Being blindfolded at the same time, the person will lead the performer to the exact spot, and the vibrations of the cord or wire by which the performer is connected to this person will speak as plainly as outspoken words.

A Simple Experiment

In your own family circle, request, by way of experiment, that someone present touch a certain article, placed amongst many others on the table, while you retire from the room. When they have done so, have yourself blindfolded, take this person by the wrist, with your fingers pressing slightly on his pulse, and, requesting him to think of nothing else but the article he touched, lead him by the hand to the table. Your will being stronger than his, he will, without really knowing it, lead you to the article he has previously touched. The sudden pause in his pulse will tell you that his hand is over the article.

This is a very simple experiment, but it speaks for itself, and by constant practice your mind and will naturally become much stronger than those of your subjects; and as your will becomes stronger, the faculty of reading other persons' thoughts will become easy for you.

Let my readers follow carefully the experiments of Mr. Irving Bishop, Mr. Stuart Cumberland, and others, and they will probably in a short time receive a practical proof that thought-reading is a genuine scientific proceeding, based upon certain natural phenomena and mental powers and faculties, as the power is latent to a greater or lesser extent in everyone, and can be fully developed by practice and culture.

Reading Papers Written by the Audience

Thought-reading of late has been carried out to a very great extent, and many experiments have been introduced that are called "thought reading," when in reality they are nothing of the kind, but simply depend upon the performer's expertise in sleight of hand. There are many methods of performing the experiment of reading papers written by the audience, but the one I intend to describe is really the best that has yet been brought before the public. At the present time there are only a few performers who adopt this particular modus operandi, which is remarkably successful. It is, however, indispensable that the performer should be very expert in sleight of hand.

The mode of working this particular trick, because it is nothing else but a trick, and not thought-reading proper, is somewhat as follows:

The performer comes forward upon the stage and, after a few suitable remarks respecting the experiment, requests some gentleman to step upon the stage to assist him. He now shows a number of slips of blank paper, about two inches long by about three-quarters of an inch in width, and hands them to the gentleman upon the stage, to distribute amongst the audience. When he goes amongst them for that purpose, and while he is distributing them, the performer requests the audience to write any particular name upon the slips of paper that their fancy may direct, but to be sure to write each name *plainly and distinctly*, so that it is readable, and, after having done so, to fold each paper up very small, so as to make a small square of it.

Those who have written on the papers are then requested to place them in a goblet, which the gentleman who handed out the papers has in his hands. After all the papers are collected in the goblet, the gentleman returns with it to the stage, and the performer, looking in the goblet, places *two fingers* in it, and draws the attention of the gentleman to the fact that some of the papers are not folded correctly.

The performer then withdraws his two fingers from the goblet, and requests the gentleman to turn all the papers out upon the table, and to screw each paper up into a small pellet; while he is doing so, the performer leaves the stage, as he tells his audience, for fear that he may be accused of trying to read the papers.

When all the papers are screwed up into pellets, the gentleman on the stage calls out "Ready," and the performer once more comes forward. He now requests the gentleman to hand him one of the papers, which he receives with the fingers of his right hand, and taking it, the performer walks down amongst his audience and hands the paper to one of them, with the request that he will open it, read the name, fold it up again as before into a pellet, and place it in the palm of his right hand, and when ready to call out.

The performer immediately returns to the stage and goes off to the side until he hears the word "Ready," at which he again comes forward and requests the person holding the paper to raise the hand containing it well up, with the knuckles toward the performer, who looks at it very intently for a second or two, and then calls out the name written upon the paper correctly, even describing any peculiarities that there may be in the shaping of the letters. The person holding the paper of course will at once declare that the word is correct, and the performer then requests the person who wrote that name to claim the paper, to see if it is the one he wrote, and which he will find is the case.

The performer then requests the gentleman on the stage to hand him a second paper, which, when it is handed to him, he immediately hands to another person in the audience, with the same request as made to the person who held the first paper. This second paper the performer reads in the same manner, and so on with the others, until they are all read, but always leaving the stage each time a paper is handed to any person in the audience until the signal word "Ready" is called out, when he comes on immediately, and stands at the front of the stage until he has read the word and described the writing accurately.

The secret of being able to read all these papers is simple enough, but it is necessary for the performer to be very expert and quick in all his movements, and above all to have a remarkably good memory.

When the papers are collected in the goblet and returned to the performer, he places two fingers into the goblet, as if to steady it while he looks inside, but in reality to secure one of the papers, which he draws out of the goblet as he withdraws his fingers. This paper he conceals immediately within his palm, at the same time requesting the gentleman to screw the papers into pellets; while this is being done, the performer goes off at the side of the stage. The moment he is off, he opens the paper he has secretly obtained possession of, and reads the name thereon, and also notices all peculiarities in the writing and shape of the letters, which he commits to memory. He then folds up the paper small, and conceals it between the first and second fingers of his right hand. When the gentleman upon the stage calls out "Ready," the performer goes on. A paper is now handed to him, which he takes, and hands *apparently* to one of the audience, but in reality he hands over the other paper which he had concealed, and which has been secretly changed by the performer in walking from the stage to the audience. The performer now goes off the stage with the paper that was handed to him by the gentleman who is assisting, and when he is off the stage he opens it and reads the name, and screws it up small again, and conceals it as before, between two fingers of the right hand. When the signal is given, the performer goes to the front of the stage, and of course reads the name written upon the first paper handed out to the audience, and which is the one he secretly obtained possession of at the outset. This performance he repeats each time a paper is given him, not handing that one out, but substituting the other paper which he has concealed, and the contents of which he knows. As the reader can judge, the performer must have a good memory, and must not confuse the names, otherwise the trick loses half its interest.

It frequently happens, when the papers are handed out to be written on, that some person, wanting to be sharper than others, will return his paper without any writing upon it, but with some peculiar mark, such as a stroke, a diamond, or a round O, or the person may even prick two or three pinholes in it. Therefore the performer must be as sharp as that person, and, in describing such papers, always name every mark upon them, even to a dirty smudge made by a person's finger. If the performer is particular in so doing, the trick will appear even more marvelous to an audience.

CHAPTER 13

CONCLUSION

It now only remains for me, in bringing this work to a conclusion, to give a few parting hints to the student.

Conjuring is an art which, like everything else, must be learned thoroughly, and the student should not attempt to perform in public until he is thoroughly proficient, and perfectly understands the working of the various tricks and illusions with which he has to deal. In getting up any trick, even the simplest, whether it involves any sleight of hand or not, the instructions should be first read carefully and diligently studied, and then practiced slowly until the working of the trick is conquered.

The student should commence with those tricks which are the simplest and easiest in the working, and having practiced these diligently until he has thoroughly mastered the working of them, he can then proceed with tricks which are more difficult to accomplish, advancing step by step from the beginning to the end.

Having mastered this portion, he should next proceed to devote himself to the study of the dramatic element, which is a very important feature in the character he has to sustain. To his audience he is apparently a person possessing supernatural powers, and he must endeavor, by words and gestures, to sustain that part, and should persuade himself that his fictitious powers are truly a reality, and that his wand is the emblem of his supernatural power.

Every performer has some peculiar style of his own, and the "patter" and talk must be suitable and appropriate for the trick he has in hand. He must not attempt to make his audience believe that he is about to do such-and-such wonderful tricks, but rather the reverse, telling them that he will introduce to their notice a few simple tricks, and when the audience are more agreeably surprised and astonished when the trick is concluded, as expecting, as they are led to suppose, to see something simple, they see something done which appears to them to be really clever.

The student must always be ready with some apt repartee in answer to his audience, and must introduce as much wit, fun, and merriment into his talk as he possibly can, in order to keep his audience in a good humor; to this end he must acquire the art of talking while working any trick, and abstain from casting his eyes downward to watch the movements of his hands. He must never tell his audience what he intends to do, as in that case, if they knew beforehand, they would direct all their vigilance to detect him in the working of the particular trick he has in hand. Some performers can, by means of their talk, so invest with importance some simple trick of parlor magic that it is raised in the estimation of the audience to the dignity of a stage trick.

In pretending to pass a coin from right to left, he should endeavor to persuade himself, for the time being, that the coin is really in his left hand, and act accordingly. In touching with his wand some piece of apparatus to effect some pretended transmission, and pronouncing the mystic word

"Pass," he should forget the expedient, for the time being, by which the result is obtained, and seek to believe that the effect is really produced by the magical process, allowing all his gestures and actions to act in accordance with this belief, thus causing the audience to imagine that such transmission has really occurred, the actions and gestures of the performer influencing and leading the imagination of the audience to this conclusion.

The student should, under all circumstances, keep his presence of mind and *never get nervous*, and above all things *take his time* and never hurry his movements, but allow the audience time to see and appreciate his various proceedings. He should be quick, without hurrying through any particular trick. *He should not make any unusual show of his dexterity*, but execute the change or pass as quietly and deliberately as he possibly can, and seek to send his audience away in the belief that no sleight of hand has been employed at all.

A performer should not try to be funny unless he is naturally so, because he might unwittingly introduce his fun at a point when or where it would not be appreciated. He may occasionally meet with people in his audience who profess to know how he does everything, and seek to embarrass him; and when he does so, if he can by any means in his power make this person look foolish, he should do so; it is seldom a very difficult matter. If he happens to make a failure, he must never plead guilty to it, but try to bring the trick to some kind of a conclusion, even though it be a weak one. He should never expose the working of any trick to the audience, as they would not really appreciate it, and its charm and novelty would henceforth be lost upon them;

besides which, he would be exposing the invention, conceived and planned by a performer cleverer than himself—
and what is invented by another person should not be
exposed to an audience. I have not written this work as an
exposé of conjuring, illusions, and so-called spiritualism,
but as a guide and manual for those who wish to study the
"dark" arts for the amusement and pleasure of others.

Many of the tricks described in this book require little or
no apparatus, while others require very expensive mechanical appliances. Some of the simpler kinds the student, if
ingenious, can make or get made himself, while the others
would have to be purchased from some conjuring emporium.

Before commencing an evening's entertainment, the student should draw up a program of the various tricks he
intends to work, for the benefit of himself and his assistants,
taking care to arrange it so that the tricks are connected in
groups. In setting his tables, he should not have a number
of superfluous articles upon them, but only a set or two of
pieces of apparatus in constant use, his assistant bringing
on the various articles or apparatus as they are required for
the different tricks, as arranged in the program. Always
arrange to have music, if possible, as the performer can, at
a certain and critical portion of a trick, divert attention
momentarily from himself to the musicians by simply asking
for a little music; and the eyes of the audience being for the
moment directed toward the player or players, the performer in that moment is able to effect without notice some
difficult change, which it would have been awkward to do if
the eyes of the audience had been fully directed toward him.

In working hat tricks, for example, by asking for music at
a certain moment, the eyes of the audience being directed

at that instant toward the musicians, the performer can introduce into the hat the articles he wishes to place there without attracting attention.

Having come to the end of my remarks and hints, I can only say that the student cannot expect to make a conjurer of himself in a month, or even a year, as it takes a great deal of practice and study before he will be thoroughly master of all the various tricks and illusions herein described.

In conclusion, I may say that the student must be armed against failure as well as prepared for success, before coming forward before the public.